Information Brokers:
Case Studies
of Successful Ventures

Information Brokers:
Case Studies
of Successful Ventures

Alice Jane Holland Johnson, MLS, BA

The Haworth Press, Inc.
New York • London • Norwood (Australia)

Information Brokers: Case Studies of Successful Ventures has also been published as *Journal of Interlibrary Loan, Document Delivery & Information Supply*, Volume 5, Number 2 1994.

The development, preparation, and publication of this work has been undertaken with great care. However, the publisher, employees, editors, and agents of The Haworth Press and all imprints of The Haworth Press, Inc., including The Haworth Medical Press and Pharmaceutical Products Press, are not responsible for any errors contained herein or for consequences that may ensue from use of materials or information contained in this work. Opinions expressed by the author(s) are not necessarily those of The Haworth Press, Inc.

The Haworth Press, Inc., 10 Alice Street, Binghamton, NY 13904-1580, USA

Library of Congress Cataloging-in-Publication Data

Johnson, Alice Jane Holland.
    Information brokers: case studies of successful ventures/Alice Jane Holland Johnson.
      p. cm.
    Includes bibliographical references.
    ISBN 1-56024-690-1
    1. Information services–United States–Case studies. I. Title
Z674.5.U5J64 1994   94-23528
025'.00973–dc20   CIP

INDEXING & ABSTRACTING

Contributions to this publication are selectively indexed or abstracted in print, electronic, online, or CD-ROM version(s) of the reference tools and information services listed below. This list is current as of the copyright date of this publication. See the end of this section for additional notes.

- *Abstracts on Sustainable Agriculture,* Deutches Zentrum fur Entwicklungs technologien, Nevenlander Weg 23, 2725 Hemslingen, Germany

- *Current Awareness Bulletin,* Association for Information Management, Information House, 20-24 Old Street, London EC1V 9AP, England

- *Index to Periodical Articles Related to Law,* University of Texas, 727 East 26th Street, Austin, TX 78705

- *Information Reports & Bibliographies,* Science Associates International, Inc., 465 West End Avenue, New York, NY 10024

- *Information Science Abstracts,* Plenum Publishing Company, 233 Spring Street, New York, NY 10013-1578

- *INSPEC Information Services,* Institution of Electrical Engineers, Michael Faraday House, Six Hills Way, Stevenage, Herts SG1 2AY, England

(continued)

- *INTERNET ACCESS (& additional networks) Bulletin Board for Libraries ("Bubl"), coverage of information resources on INTERNET, JANET, and other networks.*
  - JANET x.27: UK.AC.BATH.BUBL or 000060121.1300
  - TELNET: BUBL.BATH.AC.UK or 138.38.32.45 login 'bubl'
  - Gopher: BUBL.BATH.AC.UK. (138.32.32.45). Port 7070
  - World Wide Web: http: / / www.bubl.bath.ac.uk./BUBL/home.htm
  - NISSWAIS telnetniss.ac.uk (for the NISS gateway), The Andersonian Library, Curran Building, 101 St. James Road, Glasgow G4 0NS, Scotland

- *Library & Information Science Abstracts (LISA),* Bowker-Saur Limited, Maypole House, Maypole Road, East Grinstead, West Sussex RH19 1HH, England

- *Library Literature,* The H.W. Wilson Company, 950 University Avenue, Bronx, NY 10452

- *Newsletter of Library and Information Services,* China Sci-Tech Book Review, Library of Academia Sinica, 8 Kexueyuan Nanlu, Zhongguancun, Beijing 100080, People's Republic of China

- *Referativnyi Zhurnal (Abstracts Journal of the Institute of Scientific Information of the Republic of Russia),* The Institute of Scientific Information, Baltijskaja ul., 14, Moscow A-219, Republic of Russia

- *Sage Public Administration Abstracts (SPAA),* Sage Publications, Inc., 2455 Teller Road, Newbury Park, CA 91320

- *The Informed Librarian,* Infosources Publishing, 140 Norma Road, Teaneck, NJ 07666

(continued)

SPECIAL BIBLIOGRAPHIC NOTES

*related to special journal issues (separates)
and indexing/abstracting*

☐ indexing/abstracting services in this list will also cover material in any "separate" that is co-published simultaneously with Haworth's special thematic journal issue or DocuSerial. Indexing/abstracting usually covers material at the article/chapter level.

☐ monographic co-editions are intended for either non-subscribers or libraries which intend to purchase a second copy for their circulating collections.

☐ monographic co-editions are reported to all jobbers/wholesalers/approval plans. The source journal is listed as the "series" to assist the prevention of duplicate purchasing in the same manner utilized for books-in-series.

☐ to facilitate user/access services all indexing/abstracting services are encouraged to utilize the co-indexing entry note indicated at the bottom of the first page of each article/chapter/contribution.

☐ this is intended to assist a library user of any reference tool (whether print, electronic, online, or CD-ROM) to locate the monographic version if the library has purchased this version but not a subscription to the source journal.

☐ individual articles/chapters in any Haworth publication are also available through the Haworth Document Delivery Services (HDDS).

Information Brokers:
Case Studies of Successful Ventures

CONTENTS

Preface:
Library Science Theses

A large number of library sciences theses pass by the library profession unseen and unknown. I have attempted to "rescue" those that fall within the purview of the *Journal of Interlibrary Loan, Document Delivery & Information Supply*. Dr. Johnson's thesis, Information Brokers: Case Studies of Successful Ventures, is one that a great many librarians will find useful. If you are planning to start an information brokerage, whether as an entrepreneur or as a member of a document delivery group in a library, you will find Dr. Johnson's thesis instructive. The successful methods of the firms and librarians that Dr. Johnson has gathered can be repeated by knowledgeable professionals.

Leslie R. Morris

[Haworth indexing entry note]: "Preface: Library Science Theses," Morris, Leslie R. Published in *Information Brokers: Case Studies of Successful Ventures* (Alice Jane Holland Johnson) The Haworth Press, Inc., 1994, p. xi. Multiple copies of this article/chapter may be purchased from The Haworth Document Delivery Center [1-800-3-HAWORTH; 9:00 a.m. - 5:00 p.m. (EST)].

Acknowledgements

A project such as this could never be completed without the help and support of many individuals. You all deserve my thanks and appreciation.

I thank the members of my doctoral committee: Dr. Derrell Bulls, Dr. Ana Cleveland, Dr. Evelyn Curry, and Dr. Brooke Sheldon, with a very special thanks to my chairman, Dr. Bernie Schlessinger, who had the patience and kindness to work with me. You all gave me much needed support and encouragement.

I thank all my friends who have been there when I needed them, especially this last year. There are so many of you, and I'm grateful to you all. I particularly want to thank Metta Nicewarner, Peg Rezac, Diane Hudson, Eileen Kopp, Betty Hodge, Elizabeth Snapp, and Roslynn Seidenstein, without whose telephone calls, I'd probably still be writing Chapter II.

Thanks to my own "special librarians"–Jimmie Harris and John Hepner–who have unfailingly tracked down lost citations or elusive bits of information with a smile, and to Mary Anne Sawers for finding things for me. Very special thanks go to David Peters from the Telecommunications Department, who went above and beyond his requirements to make arrangements so I could conduct and record telephone interviews.

Many thanks to Laurie Hammett, my typist, who made sense out of my handwritten notes and who pointed out inconsistencies, misspelled words, grammatical errors, and knows *APA*! She made this writing a lot easier for me because I had confidence the typing would be done right–and it was!

Most of all, I'd like to thank my family for allowing me the time

[Haworth indexing entry note]: "Acknowledgements," Johnson, Alice Jane Holland. Published in *Information Brokers: Case Studies of Successful Ventures* (Alice Jane Holland Johnson) The Haworth Press, Inc., 1994, p. xiii-xiv. Multiple copies of this article/chapter may be purchased from The Haworth Document Delivery Center [1-800-3-HAWORTH; 9:00 a.m. - 5:00 p.m. (EST)].

away from them to do what needed to be done. Without you I couldn't have gotten through.

My gratitude goes to all of you who love me and whom I love—thank you for everything!

Alice Jane Holland Johnson

Information Brokers: Case Studies of Successful Ventures

An information broker is an individual who researches or provides other information-related services on demand and for profit. This type of free-lance library service originated on the West Coast in the early 1970s and escalated rapidly beginning in the mid-1970s. The purpose of this study was to investigate and describe brokers and to develop a model for establishing an information brokerage firm.

The case method of research was selected as the strategy for this study since the focus was on a current, real-life situation and primarily posed "how" and "why" questions, with the researcher having no control over events. One hundred twenty-five information brokers who were identified as having been in business for a minimum of 5 years were sent a questionnaire to determine their eligibility to further participate in the research, based on criteria defined by the researcher. From the 85 (68%) questionnaires returned, 6 individuals representing various sizes of firms were invited to be case study participants. The selected respondents were then interviewed, either in person or by telephone, using pre-determined questions. This interview focused on their individual characteristics and details of how they initiated their businesses. A model for establishing an information brokerage firm was then developed, based on interview responses and recommendations found in the literature.

The major findings of the study concluded that:

[Haworth co-indexing entry note]: "Information Brokers: Case Studies of Succesful Ventures." Johnson, Alice Jane Holland. Co-published simultaneously in the *Journal of Interlibrary Loan, Document Delivery & Information Supply* (The Haworth Press, Inc.) Vol. 5, No. 2, 1994, pp. 1-2; and; *Information Brokers: Case Studies of Successful Ventures* (Alice Jane Holland Johnson) The Haworth Press, Inc., 1994, pp. 1-2. Multiple copies of this article/chapter may be purchased from The Haworth Document Delivery Center [1-800-3-HAWORTH; 9:00 a.m. - 5:00 p.m. (EST)].

1. The majority of information brokerage firms were established prior to 1980 by one principal holding an M.L.S. degree.
2. Services most offered by information brokers are research, consulting, online searching, document delivery, and manual searching.
3. Most (85%) participants accept no legal responsibility for information they provide clients.
4. Case study participants generally fit the typical entrepreneurial profile.
5. Money was not the impetus for initiating or remaining in information brokering; frustration with limitations/restrictions in traditional organizations primarily affected those decisions.
6. Copyright issues were of minor concern to most respondents.
7. Information brokers surveyed did not consistently follow standard or recommended business procedures in the establishment of their companies.

Chapter I:

Introduction

"Information" is a topic widely discussed in both the popular and scholarly literature, both of which generally note that the impact of information in society is immense with far-reaching implications on the economy of the U. S. as a whole.

In 1962, economist Fritz Machlup (1962) identified over 50 information-oriented activities within 5 classes (education, communications media, research and development, information machinery, and information activities), which he used to measure the growth of the "knowledge industries." He estimated that in 1958 the knowledge industries comprised approximately 29% of the gross national product (GNP).

The business implications of Machlup's research were promoted by Peter Drucker (1968) who reported that after World War II, the United States shifted from an economy of goods to a "knowledge economy." He suggested that in 1955, one-fourth of the GNP of the United States was based on the pledge industries and that by 1965 this sector accounted for one-third of a larger economy. Harvard sociologist Daniel Bell (1973) coined the term "postindustrial economy" in 1973 to describe the evolution of advanced economies as they progressed from preindustrial to industrial, and ultimately to the postindustrial stages of development. During the final stage, Bell states, the application of knowledge and intellectual technology becomes the critical factor of production.

In 1977, *The Information Economy* by Marc U. Porat was pub-

[Haworth co-indexing entry note]: "Introduction." Johnson, Alice Jane Holland. Co-published simultaneously in the *Journal of Interlibrary Loan, Document Delivery & Information Supply* (The Haworth Press, Inc.) Vol. 5, No. 2, 1994, pp. 3-8; and; *Information Brokers: Case Studies of Successful Ventures* (Alice Jane Holland Johnson) The Haworth Press, Inc., 1994, pp. 3-8. Multiple copies of this article/chapter may be purchased from The Haworth Document Delivery Center [1-800-3-HAWORTH; 9:00 a.m. - 5:00 p.m. (EST)].

lished by the Department of Commerce. This study set up a six-sector economic model which includes both primary and secondary information products and services. It concluded that in 1967 more than 46% of the GNP and 53% of labor income was derived from knowledge, communication, and information work. The study further examined the work force from 1860 projected to 1980, concluding that in the late 1950s, the American workforce had shifted from an industrial to an information work force (Porat, 1977). It also supported the theory that the sources of wealth had changed from capital to information and knowledge resources (Marchand, 1986).

Most studies of the accelerating information economy emphasize the role of computers and technologies in the change from the industrial to the information economy. As the technologies have changed and emerged, the information business has developed more new technologies, products, and new services (Marchand, 1986). One such service being offered is that of the information broker, or fee-based information service.

The first fee-based information service in the United States, the Engineering Societies Library, was introduced in New York City in 1913 and was designed to fulfill the needs of professional engineers. The next major service was the University of New Mexico's Bureau of Business and Economic Research, established in 1945 to provide business, economic and demographic information to the University and to private organizations. Both of these services were non-profit and fee-based. In 1958, World Wide Information Services, a commercial news service for journalists, began in New York City (Maranjian, 1980). This and most subsequent information services, regardless of size, have been organized to generate a profit.

Another important development occurred in 1969, when Andrew Garvin founded Information Clearinghouse, Incorporated, which conducts business as FIND/SVP in New York City and is affiliated with the Parisian S'il Vous Plait, begun in 1948 as a telephone service offering information on any subject for a fee. S'il Vous Plait has offices in major cities throughout the world, and FIND/SVP has become the largest information brokerage firm in the United States.

The early 1970s saw the rise of free-lancers belonging to the grass-roots "Alternatives to Librarianship" movement originating on the West Coast (predominantly in the San Francisco Bay Area). But the proliferation of information brokers really began in the mid-1970s (Maranjian, 1980). According to Martin White, this movement came in response to the economic upheaval caused by the Seven Days War in the Middle East, when companies were analyzing their operations to find ways of reducing overhead. The requisite cut-backs precipitated the closing of library and information centers associated with these companies at a time when economics dictated a corporate need to diversify into new markets and products which in turn required information. Simultaneously, on-line access to bibliographic databases became readily available through Lockheed and System Development Corporation, allowing freelance librarians to do literature searches that were time- and cost-effective without the need for a major library (White, 1981). This combination of circumstances made the time right for librarians to develop the innovative career concept of information brokering.

Information brokering is often an attractive alternative to traditional librarianship. There is frequently less job security in information brokering–unknown salary and lack of benefits, for example–but it allows a different avenue of pursuit for people whose jobs have been eliminated or who have relocated where employment is not available or who did not find a position after library school. Many individuals feel an increased sense of professional accomplishment when they are successful in running an information brokerage firm. Through brokering, they also can avoid having to contend with the politics of positions in institutional settings. Information brokering satisfies people having a need for achievement, and it offers variety and the excitement of ever-shifting challenges (O'Leary, 1987).

STATEMENT OF PURPOSE

The purpose of the study was to investigate and describe characteristics of successful information brokers and information brokerage firms and develop a model for establishing an information brokerage firm.

STATEMENT OF THE PROBLEM

Librarians have long held a traditional role in society. They could specialize in particular types of libraries, e.g., public, academic, school or special libraries, but they generally remained in an institutional setting of one kind or another. With the increasingly rapid movement into the information age and subsequent development of accessible secondary information sources, combined with a reduced job market for librarians, a new entrepreneurial spirit began to emerge in the mid-1970s, and information brokers became an integral part of the information industry in the United States.

Since the 1970s, numerous librarians have inaugurated fee-based services either as a full-time occupation, or as a means to supplement their incomes on a part-time basis. The general perception of why few of these businesses have survived centers around the fact that these entrepreneurs, although possessing adequate library and information skills, lack business acumen. But little hard data exist to support these perceptions.

This study identified those specific skills associated with the establishment and success of information brokerage firms, and developed a model for establishing an information brokerage firm.

RATIONALE FOR THE STUDY

The intent of this study was to identify specific skills and relevant characteristics required to establish a successful information brokerage firm and to develop a model to assist individuals in the process of undertaking an information brokerage firm as a viable business venture.

DEFINITIONS

For the purpose of the study, the following definitions were used:

1. *Information broker*–an individual who researches or provides other information-related services on demand and for profit. Alternative titles for information broker include independent

information specialist, information specialist, information professional, and freelance librarian.
2. *Information brokerage firm*–a company, or organization which provides the services of an information broker.
3. *Entrepreneur*–the organizer of an enterprise, particularly one who owns, manages, and assumes the risks involved with the business.

Success, for the purpose of this study, is measured by the following criteria:

1. The company is currently operational and has been for a minimum of five years.
2. Principals (owners/managers) of the company each net what she/he considers an adequate annual salary.
3. The information brokerage firm provides full-time employment for the principals of the company.

RESEARCH QUESTIONS

1. What are the characteristics of successful information brokers?
   - What are their educational backgrounds?
   - What are their work experiences?
   - Do they have a high level of drive and personal energy?
   - Do they have a high level of self-confidence?
   - Are they money-motivated?
   - Do they need positive and definite feedback?
   - Do they use past failures to their benefit?
   - Are they goal-setters?
   - Do they have a high need for achievement?
   - Do they feel they control their own destinies?
   - Do they take initiative in situations?
   - Do they seek personal responsibility?
   - Are they moderate risk-takers?
   - Do they compete against self-imposed standards?
   - Do they have an intense level of determination?
   - Do they like to see jobs to completion?

- Are they problem solvers?
- Do they know where, when, and how to ask for help?
2. What are the criteria for establishing a successful information brokerage firm?
    - How should a market survey be done to determine the need for the business?
    - What should be the target market?
    - What is critical to the initial planning stages?
        a. getting advice from a banker?
        b. retaining an attorney?
        c. hiring an accountant?
        d. developing a business plan?
    - What venture capital is required?
    - What is the anticipated level of cash flow?
    - What equipment is necessary?
    - What inventory (core resources) such as periodical subscriptions, loose-leaf services, books, and software, is needed?
    - What staffing is required?

LIMITATIONS/DELIMITATIONS

This study was limited to:

1. Brokers in the United States who have been in business a minimum of five years.
2. Brokerage firms initiated by an individual who is still actively involved in the business.
3. Information brokers with an ALA-accredited M.L.S. degree.
4. Privately-held businesses; it will not include fee-based services provided by public, academic, or special libraries, or those affiliated with any other organization.

Chapter II:

Review of the Literature

Information brokering, as an identifiable profession, began in the mid-1970s. Warnken's *Directory of Fee-Based Information Services* (1978) lists 177 information brokers in the United States. Helen Burwell's *Directory of Fee-Based Information Services* (1987) notes 447 entries, an increase of 153%. Only 24 (14%) businesses listed in the 1978 edition were extant in 1987, indicating that the life-span of information brokering firms is relatively brief, at least to this point in time.

BACKGROUND WORKS

An examination of the literature published from 1972 forward reveals that no in-depth case studies of information brokering firms have been reported. The search of the literature was accomplished by online searches on the topic of information brokers performed on *Library and Information Science Abstracts, Library Literature, ABI/Inform, Dissertation Abstracts International, ERIC,* and *Business Periodicals Index.* Additionally, manual searches were done in *Library Literature, Library and Information Science Abstracts,* and *Business Periodicals Index.*

Several works contain critical background material for understanding the information industry. Foremost is Fritz Malchup's *The*

[Haworth co-indexing entry note]: "Review of the Literature." Johnson, Alice Jane Holland. Co-published simultaneously in the *Journal of Interlibrary Loan, Document Delivery & Information Supply* (The Haworth Press, Inc.) Vol. 5, No. 2, 1994, pp. 9-22; and; *Information Brokers: Case Studies of Successful Ventures* (Alice Jane Holland Johnson) The Haworth Press, Inc., 1994, pp. 9-22. Multiple copies of this article/chapter may be purchased from The Haworth Document Delivery Center [1-800-3-HAWORTH; 9:00 a.m. - 5:00 p.m. (EST)].

Production and Distribution of Knowledge in the United States (1962) in which he states that "the production of knowledge is an economic activity, an industry" (p. 9). Malchup made the first attempt to measure the growth of the "knowledge industry" which he divided into education, research and development, communications media, information machinery, and information activities. Within these five broad categories he identified over 50 separate activities. Malchup estimated that in 1958 the total knowledge-production activities accounted for nearly 29% of the adjusted GNP and that "in recent years knowledge has been growing faster than the GNP" (p. 362), implying that its share of the GNP has increased.

Another important work is *The Age of Discontinuity* by Peter Drucker (1962) which defines knowledge as "systematic, purposeful, organized information" (p. 40). It presents the theory that after World War II the economy of the United States shifted from an economy of goods to an economy of knowledge; further, that "knowledge has become the central capital, the cost center, and the crucial resource of the economy. This changes labor forces and work, teaching and learning, and the meaning of knowledge and its politics" (preface, xi). According to Drucker, while the "knowledge industries" accounted for approximately 25% of the Gross National Product in 1955, by 1965 the knowledge sector accounted for one third of a much larger national product. He predicted that by the end of the 1970s it would account for one half of the GNP: every other dollar earned and spent would be earned by producing and distributing ideas and information and would be spent on obtaining ideas and information (p. 263).

Harvard sociologist Daniel Bell, in a third important study, *The Coming of Post-Industrial Society* (1973), supports the concept of the information economy. He divides societies into three economic categories: pre-industrial–mining, fishing, forestry, and agriculture; industrial–goods-producing; and post-industrial–services (pp. 126-127). As these societal stages have evolved in the United States, the shift from goods production to a predominantly service economy has occurred (p. 129). Agreeing with Malchup, Bell states that

the post-industrial society is a knowledge society in two ways: first, sources of innovation are increasingly derived from research and development and secondly, the weight of the society, measured by a larger proportion of Gross National Product and a larger share of employment, is increasingly in the knowledge field. (p. 212)

In a fourth background work published in 1977 under the aegis of the United States Department of Commerce, Marc Porat (1977) presented the report *The Information Economy: Definition and Measurement*. The study, which used a computer model for the year 1967, supported both Bell's and Malchup's theories. Porat defined information as "data that have been organized and communicated. The information *activity* includes all the resources consumed in producing, processing and distributing information goods and services" (Vol. 1, p. 2). Porat divided information activities into a "primary information sector where information is exchanged as a commodity, and the secondary information sector where information is embedded in some other good or service and not explicitly exchanged" (Vol. 1, p. 2). He concluded that in 1967, 46% of the Gross National Product was involved in information activity, and about half the labor force was in an information-related job, earning 53% of labor income (Vol. 1, p. 1). This figure approximates Drucker's prediction published five years earlier.

In the fifth major background work, John Naisbitt's *Megatrends* (1982), it is noted that by 1979 more than 60% of the population held an information-related job (p. 14). He states, "knowledge is now the driving force of our economy; the new source of power is information in the hands of many" (p. 16).

PRESENT STATUS OF THE INFORMATION ECONOMY

The results of the literature search indicate that the information economy is a reality. This economy has been the result of enormously successful adaptations of developing technologies, beginning in the 1940s and early 1950s with the development of digital computers. The new technologies called for a reappraisal of methods used for content analysis of documents and subject headings. As a result, the use of controlled vocabularies was introduced during the 1950s as were thesauruses and other hierarchical vocabularies (Salton, 1987).

With the Russian launching of Sputnik I in 1957, the scientific and technical communities, including abstracting and indexing services, came under pressure in the rapidly changing environment, to process the massive number of documents produced. Federal funding for research and development as well as product and process improvements became readily available. New products and services were developed, creating new markets. Existing services were forced to reevaluate their philosophies and products. The high level of Federal involvement ended with the 1960s, but the impetus needed for acquiring additional and more effective services remained (Cooper & Lunin, 1982). One such class of services revolved around database production and use. According to Neufeld and Cornog (1986): "the most important phenomenon in the information industry has been the emergence and popularity of machine-readable databases. In fact, databases can almost be said to have created the information industry as we now know it" (p. 183).

Bibliographic databases originated in the mid-1960s, as abstracting and indexing services moved toward computerized photocomposition using magnetic tape. The National Library of Medicine was running on-demand searches by 1964; *Chemical Abstracts Services* products became available for computer searching on magnetic tape by 1965. Other abstracting and indexing services quickly made themselves available in order to stay competitive (Neufeld & Cornog, 1986, p. 183).

The years 1970-1975 saw a change from batch searching to online searching; during this time most major abstracting and indexing services began to computerize to decrease production costs and time lags for print products. For-profit companies such as Data Courier and Predicast entered the market, producing databases as well as print products. These databases were sold, leased, and/or offered through information utilities such as Dialog or SDC. Consequently, by the mid-1970s, the information industry recognized the "online revolution" (Neufeld & Cornog, 1986).

The continued growth and development of the information industry in the United States can be partially attributed to other factors in addition to early government assistance. For example, telecommunications services are not under government control, but the competition between companies in this area has promoted the development of increasingly sophisticated services at lower charges. Another important factor is the size and homogeneity of the market. There are more than 3 million businesses in the United States, all of which share one common language and have access to standardized electrical voltages, frequencies, and plugs (White, 1981, p. 3). Still another factor is the cohesiveness of the information industry, fostered by the Information Industry Association, founded in 1968 for the purpose of representing the interests of the industry in government and to act as a forum for the providers and users of information services and products (White, 1981, p. 4).

The information industry, as a whole, represents diverse businesses which emphasize large scale production. It encompasses such areas as database production and publishing, business information, computer software, publishing, electronic publishing, database distributors, financial markets information, directing publishing, market research, consulting, indexing and index publishing as well as other services less heavily used (Warner, 1987, p. 13).

INFORMATION BROKERAGES

Information brokering firms are a specialized segment of the information industry providing information services on a profit-making basis. These companies offer a wide variety of services: online searching, document delivery, research, consulting, compiling bibliographies, indexing, manual searching, custom information service, current awareness, abstracting, education and training, editing, library development, library services, and cataloging (Warner, 1987, p. 11).

The fee-based information services established prior to 1950 were primarily related to specific research needs in science and technology and were affiliated with academic institutions (Maranjian & Boss, 1980, p. 5). During the 1960s, fee-based services began to increase to meet industrial demands. The real surge of information brokers, as noted in the introduction, occurred in the 1970s, originating on the West Coast, particularly in the San Francisco Bay Area (Maranjian & Boss, 1980, p. 6). One explanation for the growth of fee-based information services during this era is offered by Betty Eddison who stated that "with the election of

President Nixon (in 1972), the bottom fell out of the library market" (Pemberton & Gordon, 1986, p. 13). The continuing trend of information brokering as a career may be attributed both to the rise of entrepreneurship in the United States and to the variety, excitement, and change available to individuals engaged in such an occupation.

Information brokers can be useful to numerous broad-based clients who have general or specialized information needs. One example of this is given by Carol Johnson (1987), who reports that marketing research is essential to the marketing process. Since skill, experience, and training are mandatory for retrieving information successfully and economically from secondary research, she recommends the use of information brokers, especially for independent marketing research firms, marketing consultants, and free-lancers who do not have access to a corporate library. She states that information brokers can obtain information from commercial databases which can indicate "relevant theories, concepts, models and experts. They can also identify new markets and opportunities, pinpoint trends, patterns, consumer tastes and habits, assist in developing new products and brands, and track competitors" (Johnson, 1987, p. 14).

Another example of information broker use is given by M. L. Johnson (1987), who contends that the role of an information broker "is comparable to any other broker in a competitive environment. The only difference is that the product is information. Information is researched, purchased, packaged and distributed to a select clientele for a fee" (p. 3).

The literature indicates that information brokers must possess certain characteristics, characteristics which are frequently common to experienced librarians. Maxine Davis (1976) compiled a list based on her own experiences as an information broker:

1. Understand the power of information.
2. Ability to understand the actual needs of the client, not necessarily those which are stated.
3. Skill in interviewing, listening, communicating.
4. Adaptability to new situations.
5. Ability to organize concepts as well as things.

6. Ability to synthesize information.
7. Ability to interpret information and repackage it.
8. Ability to train and work with non-library-oriented staff.
9. Administrative ability and business expertise.
10. Research experience.
11. Ability to interact with databases.
13. Ability to work independently (p. 18).

Martin White (1981) reproduced the preceding list and added two more essential qualities: "the ability to take advice as well as give it; to have pride in the quality of work produced" (p. 21).

Due to the nature of information brokering, an individual engaged in the occupation is usually considered to be an entrepreneur. According to Albert King (1985):

> Independent business is an appealing occupation. Being one's own boss offers independence, personal satisfaction, profit expectations, and social involvement. Entrepreneurship is not for everybody. The individual who desires job stability and security may find owning a business to be unbearable. The decision to go into business for oneself must be made in an objective, deliberate, and comprehensive manner. It is necessary to evaluate the pros and cons of a particular business venture. A well-thought-out decision process coupled with a heightened awareness of one's own personality traits is believed to enhance greatly the probability of entrepreneurial success. (p. 400)

Researchers have found the personality of an entrepreneur to be a primary indicator to success or failure. The following dominant characteristics are most often identified with successful entrepreneurs (Timmons, 1979):

1. Entrepreneurs are recognized as having a high level of drive and personal energy.
2. Successful entrepreneurs have a high level of self-confidence.
3. Entrepreneurs view money as a way of keeping score.
4. Entrepreneurs have a strong need for positive and definite feedback.

5. Effective entrepreneurs use past failures to their benefit.
6. The successful entrepreneur has the ability and the commitment to set clear goals.
7. Entrepreneurs have an insatiable drive for accomplishment.
8. Entrepreneurs believe they can control their own destinies.
9. The successful entrepreneur takes initiative and seeks personal responsibility.
10. Entrepreneurs prefer to take moderate, calculated risks.
11. High-performing entrepreneurs continuously compete against self-imposed standards.
12. Entrepreneurs have an intense level of determination and desire to solve problems and complete the job.
13. Entrepreneurs who are successful know when, where, and how to seek help (p. 199).

According to John Burch (1986), entrepreneurs like independence, want to be their own bosses, are self-governing, are loners and individualists, and like to make their own decisions. He agrees that entrepreneurs possess common personality traits. His list includes:

1. a desire to achieve
2. hard work
3. nurturing quality (i.e., taking charge of and watching over a venture until it can stand alone)
4. acceptance of responsibility
5. reward orientation (receiving monetary, recognition, or respect)
6. optimism
7. orientation to excellence
8. organization
9. profit orientation (serving as a gauge of achievement and performance) (p. 15).

The literature has descriptions of various information brokerages. Five of these were selected by the writer and are reviewed below.

Georgia Finnegan, in a 1976 *Special Libraries* article, describes the founding of Information Unlimited, a free-lance information service located in Berkeley, California. The idea for the company originated with Sue Rugge in 1971 when she realized that people who no longer had access to special libraries still needed literature searches and other library-related services. As a special librarian she felt there might be many small companies needing the services of a librarian but unable to hire one on a full-time basis. Finnegan, also a special librarian, expressed an interest in providing services to a wider clientele; the two women collaborated on the idea, and the business became a reality.

Finnegan and Rugge began by cultivating previous library and business contacts, guaranteeing a 24 to 48 hour turnaround for obtaining documents. Nearly half of the business done by Information Unlimited came from special libraries. Company staff members used resources from local universities to fill requests. Items not locally available were verified, checked in union lists, and sent to other libraries.

Another service offered clients by Information Unlimited was literature searching on Dialog. Still other services included organizing libraries, records management, market surveys, and directory publication. Research services and literature searching were charged on an hourly basis at $12.50 per hour.

The company began with no funding or capital investment–billings paid all expenses. Various direct costs such as telephone bills and postage were billed back to clients to minimize overhead. In 1976 the staff consisted of 4 full-time and 9 part-time employees plus 6 people working in the field and contract workers hired on an as-needed basis (Finnegan, 1976, pp. 102-103).

According to a June, 1985 article appearing in *Sales and Marketing Management,* Rugge's company is now Information on Demand (IOD) and has 70 full-time employees handling over 500 requests daily, with earnings in excess of $2 million annually. There are no monthly fees or retainers and estimates are given on research projects, with report costs averaging $200 to $400. Document delivery is $14 per item for up to 20 photocopied pages; copyright royalties and postage are included in the price.

Approximately 75% of the business was document delivery, with the remainder being literature searching, current awareness, indexing, market research, and translation. Document delivery alone had nearly doubled from the previous year–up to 10,000 requests monthly. The increase is attributed to companies' ability to order documents through Dialog's DIALORDER. Turnaround time will probably be reduced in the near future with the installation of an electronic network connecting field staff to the main office. There is a staff of 29 at Berkeley, with another 17 scattered around the United States acting as "runners" to various major universities and public libraries. When an article cannot be obtained after 2 or 3 tries, the author of the article is contacted directly. In the experience of Information on Demand, authors usually respond to requests and even though offered remuneration, they frequently provide materials free of charge. Most clients at Information on Demand are large corporate libraries such as IBM which have diverse needs and feel that IOD can provide certain services, such as document delivery, more cost-effectively than traditional library services (Lesser, 1982, pp. 12, 13).

The second information brokerage reviewed here, The Information Store in downtown San Francisco, is Georgia Finnigan's new venture. This company is primarily interested in market studies and legal research. Most work is charged on an hourly basis with bids put out on specific projects. Less than half the company's revenues are generated by document delivery. Manual and online searching are emphasized, as are publishing efforts. The staff is comparable to that of Information on Demand, but "runners" are less frequently used, and the staff generally have both library skills and business training (Lesser, 1982, p. 13).

The third information brokerage, Warner-Eddison Associates, based in Lexington, Massachusetts, was founded in 1973 by Alice Sizer Warner and Elizabeth Bole Eddison, both graduates of Simmons College. In preparation for their start-up, the two women went to the Small Business Administration where they were assigned a SCORE (Service Corps of Retired Executives) advisor who provided them with literature on entrepreneurship and small businesses. After deciding on a name for the company, Warner and Eddison retained a lawyer, registered their company name at the Town Hall, signed a partnership agreement, and opened a bank account. Deciding no one would take them seriously if they had a "kitchen table business," they decided to rent an office and engage a telephone answering service. Additionally, they hired a Certified

Public Accountant and registered their logo as a trademark (Warner, 1975).

Warner-Eddison spent over 20% of its capital for advertising, which included a high quality brochure. Both principals of the company maintained affiliation with professional library associations, to provide visibility and validity. They gave speeches to increase their exposure and had a column in a local business newspaper (Warner, 1975). Other contacts were made through the Greater Boston Chamber of Commerce and the Information Industry Association (Fragasso, 1978).

Charges were determined by the new organization on a pre-bid lump-sum basis, with the first interview free. If a job was large and not well-defined, work was done from a preliminary purchase order, with subsequent charges spelled out. Two rate schedules were used, one for profitmaking institutions and a lower one for non-profit organizations such as libraries. Warner-Eddison deliberately bid low on some jobs which offered high visibility or publicity value, a move which proved very beneficial.

The company's resources consisted of a small in-house reference library, extensive vertical files, long-distance telephone calls, and the resources of academic libraries and public libraries in the area. Networking with special libraries in the Boston area provided additional resources.

Staff consisted largely of trained professional librarians with subject specialties. As of 1975, all librarians were hired only for specific tasks on a subcontracting basis, and the only permanent help was secretarial (Warner, 1975).

A large percentage of Warner-Eddison's business was in the area of information retrieval–both manual and online, particularly in the fields of science, technology, and marketing analysis. They created and maintained corporate libraries and offered a variety of services including indexing, microfilming, and records management (Fragasso, 1978, p. 10). By 1979 the firm's services had expanded into development of management information systems for libraries and technical information centers (Holmes, 1979, p. 13).

To meet the cataloging needs of clients, Warner-Eddison developed a software package to accommodate a variety of cataloging activities. Clients initiated requests to purchase the software named

INMAGIC–a database creation and retrieval program. The previously all-service organization now had a product which required funding and a different level of support and marketing. Since funding sources traditionally do not support consulting companies, Warner and Eddison decided to split the product, INMAGIC, into a company called Inmagic, Inc., which began operations as of January 1, 1984 with Betty Eddison as chairman. Warner-Eddison Associates remains as a corporate entity, but is inactive (Pemberton & Jordon, 1986, pp. 16, 17). Alice Warner currently operates from her home as The Information Guild. Most of her activities center on writing, teaching, lecturing, and consulting on business start-ups (Warner, 1987, p. xi).

The fourth information brokerage, the largest in the United States, FIND/SVP, was incorporated in 1969 by Andrew Garvin, Haines B. Gaffner, and Kathleen Bingham. Garvin had previously been in publishing and served as a member of *Newsweek's* editorial staff in Paris, where he came in contact with the information service SVP and conceived the idea of modifying its operations to the U.S. market. He negotiated an exclusive franchise to apply SVP techniques in Canada and the United States. Gaffner had been with Business International for 10 years, a firm which gathers information and disseminates it via newsletters, reports, and briefings. Bingham had done market research for 10 years and had her own company which provided free-lance research services.

The three set up FIND/SVP as a low investment project whose business was to answer questions. According to Gaffner, the 4 most important assets of the company are:

1. A proprietary index to sources of information modeled on one developed by SVP.
2. A link to the international SVP network for getting answers to questions.
3. An extensive in-house collection of resources.
4. Reciprocal agreements with information centers and source-collection agencies which provide that an organization will share its resources upon request. The primary participants are special libraries throughout the country.

FIND's clientele covers a wide range of business interests and the in-house library's core collection reflects this diversity. The collection includes directories, dictionaries, encyclopedias, government documents, and company files. There is also a large collection of technical journals, buyers' guides, and market research reports. Trade publications are added as the need arises. The library has an extensive vertical file containing tearsheets, newspaper and journal clippings, bibliographies and government statistics (Feverstein & Mishkoff, 1976, p. 4).

Interestingly, research staff at FIND/SVP are often selected because they have no expertise in information science. The company believes that bright generalists are the best candidates for this type of work. They frequently hire liberal arts graduates as well as subject specialists and provide intensive 6 to 8 week training courses for all new employees (Doebler, 1974, p. 40). About two-thirds of the staff have graduate degrees in Library Science (Feverstein & Mishkoff, 1976, p. 5).

Rates are charged by subscription levels. When a subscriber begins the service, FIND surveys the anticipated information needs of the subscribing organization and proposes an initial monthly fee which is in effect for three months. FIND monitors use of the service during this period and renegotiates the rate to reflect actual use of the service. Usage continues to be monitored periodically to allow for further adjustments. Billing is based on units used, with units being assigned according to staff time utilized and complexity of the question (Doebler, 1972).

FIND fills over 6,000 requests per month, providing clients with facts, lists, statistics, bibliographies, literature searches, definitions, and market data. it also provides document delivery, back issues of journals, catalogs, reports, and studies (Burroughs Clearing House, 1973, p. 30). FIND publishes *The Information Catalog* quarterly which contains studies, reports, surveys, and reference books available through FIND. It is compiled by the Information Products Division and is used primarily as a marketing tool. Publications generated by FIND are separate from their contract projects; projects done for clients are resold only with permission from the client after completion of the project. Publications not authored by FIND but available for purchase through them are also offered in *The Information Catalog* (Felicetti, 1979, pp. 11, 12).

FIND has an active advertising campaign including newspaper

advertisements in the *New York Times* and the *Wall Street Journal* as well as advertisements in professional and trade journals. A blue logo is used on all promotional literature and forms; brochures are graphically innovative. Inducements are used to gain client referrals, followed up by sales calls. FIND has held databank seminars co-sponsored by database producers for management executives, designed to acquaint executives with all aspects of online information retrieval (Maranjian & Boss, 1980, p. 70).

The fifth representative firm, packaged facts, is a smaller information brokerage firm, which was established in New York City in 1960 by former marketing executive David Weiss. The company initially offered historical clipping research to assist clients in measuring the impact of product announcements or in monitoring competitor's activities. The clippings led to a tear-sheet service for advertisements, designed to locate and provide copies of all advertisements of a product or service. The work is methodical and labor-intensive, involving a systematic search of newspapers and magazines.

Most clients are from marketing and advertising companies. Approximately 85% of new business is generated from referrals from clients and from other information services, with other business coming from Yellow Pages advertising. Rates are determined on a cost plus profit margin basis. The firm currently repackages previous studies for distribution through FIND, to whom it pays a percentage of the sales price (Maranjian & Boss, 1980, pp. 82, 85, 86).

Packaged Facts provides comprehensive market study reports ranging in price from $3,500 to $15,000 for custom-prepared studies. Previously prepared studies cost $750-$1,500. The company can provide clients with raw market data or analyze information into a specialized report which recommends whether or not the company should enter a particular market and/or introduce a particular product. Data used for the report are provided to the client. The most highly specialized and analytical market probe costs $7,500-$25,000 and requires two to three months. Other services offered by Packaged Facts include document delivery, information on demand, manual searching, and online searching.

Chapter III:

Methodology

RESEARCH METHOD

The case study method, which in the judgment of the researcher and her committee, offered a viable avenue for research on the topic of information brokers, was used in this study. According to Yin (1984), "In general, case studies are the preferred strategy when 'how' or 'why' questions are being posed, when the investigator has little control over events, and when the focus is on a contemporary phenomenon within some real-life context" (p. 13).

It should be pointed out that there are criticisms of the case study method. Yin (1984) discusses traditional prejudices against this research method, and he points out that the "biased views of the investigator may influence the direction of findings and conclusions" (p. 21). Another concern is the belief that case studies "provide little basis for scientific generalization" (p. 21).

Although there are some critics of the method, there are many proponents as well. Galvin (1973) advocates the use of case studies in education for librarianship. He notes that "the descriptive case study is employed in many disciplines as a tool of inductive investigation" (p. 11). He also discusses limitations of the descriptive case study. Specifically, he states that "In the selection, organization and reporting of data, the casewriter's subjective preferences, prejudices and judgments will, inevitably, reduce the objectivity of the resulting case report (p. 255).

[Haworth co-indexing entry note]: "Methodology." Johnson Alice Jane Holland. Co-published simultaneously in the *Journal of Interlibrary Loan, Document Delivery & Information Supply* (The Haworth Press, Inc.) Vol. 5, No. 2, 1994, pp. 23-26; and; *Information Brokers: Case Studies of Successful Ventures* (Alice Jane Holland Johnson) The Haworth Press, Inc., 1994, pp. 23-26. Multiple copies of this article/chapter may be purchased from The Haworth Document Delivery Center [1-800-3-HAWORTH; 9:00 a.m. - 5:00 p.m. (EST)].

23

Busha and Harter (1980) state that:

> the case study is an appropriate type of inquiry when the investigator is interested in a single research object and attempts to alter extensive data about it so that relationships among variables associated with the observed phenomenon can be identified. (p. 151)

Towle (1954) concurs with the validity of using the case study as a research tool in his recommendation that the researcher should "concentrate on collecting and analyzing cases concerned with a particular kind of issue or problem, with the specific objective of developing a better understanding of the problem (p. 225).

POPULATION

The Directory of Fee-Based Services (1987), which contains 447 listings, was used to identify the 125 information brokers who had been in business for a minimum of five years and who offered diversified services to their clients. Each information broker was sent a questionnaire (Appendix A) to collect the desired data to determine the list of brokers to approach for the interview which would be used to write the case studies.

The questionnaires were mailed on the first of April, with an additional mailing on May 15 to those who did not respond to the first request. Of the 125 questionnaires sent, 85 (68%) were returned. The percentage of returns was surprisingly high considering the general perception of information brokers is that they are often reluctant to share information about themselves.

The questionnaire covered several broad areas. Questions 1-3 determined the establishment and form of the company. Question 4 asked for the preferred title of the respondent. Questions 5 and 6 concerned compensation and employment status (i.e., full-time or part-time). Questions 7-9 dealt with other staff employed by the firm. Question 10 asked for degrees/experience of the principal of the company, while question 11 listed possible services offered by the firm. Questions 12-15 requested brief descriptions of typical projects completed by the information brokerage firm, how many requests are handled per month, sources for information used by the company, and whether the firm assumes legal liability for the accuracy of information provided to clients. Question 16 asked what new services were being planned by the firm and Question 17 asked for the individual's perception of the future of information brokering.

The responses to the questionnaire were analyzed and tabulated. The responses were also used to collect participants for interview according to the following criteria:

1. The respondent had to be the original principal in the firm.
2. The respondent had to hold an M.L.S. degree.
3. The respondent had to feel that he/she was adequately compensated by the business.
4. The business had to provide full-time employment for the principal.

The information brokers who met the criteria for possible inclusion in the study were then further divided by company size based on employee count. Two companies were selected from each of three sizes: small, 1 to 5 employees; medium, 6 to 25 employees; large, 26 or more employees.

PROCEDURES

Principals of the selected companies were contacted and appointments set up for interviews. The interviews were conducted during July and August of 1988: one was in person, the others were by telephone. In general, the interviews varied in length from 1 to 1 1/2 hours. All were tape recorded with prior permission from the respondents. A set of questions developed prior to the interviews (a copy of the questions is included as Appendix B) provided the framework for the interviews. The questions focused on three areas: personal characteristics of the interviewee, procedures used in establishing the business, and items of a general nature concerning information brokering. Participants were encouraged to address other issues and expand on their answers as they wished.

Tapes made of the conversations with participants were reviewed extensively and case studies were prepared using information provided by the six individuals selected for this study. Responses are included as Appendix C. The results from analysis of the questionnaire and the case studies are presented in Chapter IV.

Chapter IV:

Results and Discussion

RESULTS FROM THE QUESTIONNAIRES

The Directory of Fee-Based Services (1987) was used to identify 125 information brokers who had remained in business for at least five years. A questionnaire designed to obtain the necessary data was developed and mailed. Of the 125 questionnaires mailed, 85 (68%) were returned fully or partially answered. Of those questionnaires returned, 2 respondents stated they were currently inactive, and 4 indicated they were no longer involved with information brokering because of retirement, starting another type of business, or joining another company. The final count of usable questionnaires was 63%.

The results from the questionnaire are presented below. It should be noted that not all percentages in the tables presented total 100% since some respondents gave more than one answer in appropriate situations.

Table 1 presents data obtained from question 1 which asked the date of establishment of each company.

Table 1 indicates that the largest number of information brokerage firms was formed from 1976 to 1980, the second largest firm was established during the 1981 to 1985 period. This supports Maranjian and Boss (1980) who stated that the largest number of information services started in the 1970s (p. 6). Since the survey

[Haworth co-indexing entry note]: "Results and Discussion." Johnson, Alice Jane Holland. Co-published simultaneously in the *Journal of Interlibrary Loan, Document Delivery & Information Supply* (The Haworth Press, Inc.) Vol. 5, No. 2, 1994, pp. 27-46; and; *Information Brokers: Case Studies of Successful Ventures* (Alice Jane Holland Johnson) The Haworth Press, Inc., 1994, pp. 27-46. Multiple copies of this article/chapter may be purchased from The Haworth Document Delivery Center [1-800-3-HAWORTH; 9:00 a.m. - 5:00 p.m. (EST)].

TABLE 1. Establishment of Companies

Date of Establishment	Number of Companies	Percentage of Companies
1955-1969	6	8
1970-1975	10	14
1976-1980	32	45
1981-1985	23	32
1986-	0	0

was limited to companies that were believed to have been established for at least 5 years, the reported percentages are probably lower than they would have been if questionnaire respondents had not been screened prior to any mailings.

Table 2 gives the data from question 2 which asked who initially established the business.

As shown in Table 2, the majority (78%) of information brokerage firms were initiated by the original principal of the business. Only 8% began business with a partner, and according to results of the questionnaire, these partnerships have frequently changed or dissolved completely. In the table, "Other" usually represents a person who has bought an existing information brokerage firm or has branched out into a new venture after working for an established company. Such an overwhelming majority of respondents initiating the business supports John Burch's contention that entrepreneurs like independence, want to be their own bosses, are loners and individualists, and like to make their own decisions (p. 15).

Table 3 presents the data on the current organizational structure of each company.

The three structures in Table 3 deserve some explanation. In a sole proprietorship, one person owns the business. Income from this type of organization is reported by the individual for tax purposes. Income in a partnership is not taxed; it goes to the partners who handle their own shares. Assets and liabilities are also shared equally, and each partner is equally responsible for losses or suits brought against the business. In a corporation, the corporation pays the principals employed in the business a salary, and distributes any

TABLE 2. Person Initiating Establishment of Company

Response	Number of Respondents	Percentage of Respondents
Self	57	78
Jointly	6	8
Other	11	15

TABLE 3. Organizational Structure of Companies

Response	Number of Respondents	Percentage of Respondents
Sole proprietorship	39	53
Partnership	5	7
Corporation	29	39
Other	1	1

profits to other shareholders who report the income on their personal tax returns. A corporation is a separate entity which pays a higher tax rate than a sole proprietorship or a partnership. The corporation limits the personal liability of its shareholders to their investments and is also entitled to deduct expenses not allowed to other organizational forms (Maranjian & Boss, p. 60).

Over half (53%) of the respondents remain as sole proprietors, again upholding Burch's theory that entrepreneurs prefer to be independent. These figures are also consistent with those presented by Maranjian and Boss (pp. 59-60), who show that the majority of information brokers operate as sole proprietors or corporations rather than partnerships.

Table 4 tabulates the titles by which company principals prefer to be called.

In this survey 30% of respondents preferred to be known as information specialists, while 20% chose the title information broker. It is interesting to note that the title "information broker" has been in dispute since the term came into general use in the 1970s. According to Kelly Warnken (1981), the confusion over

TABLE 4. Titles Preferred by Company Principal

Titles	Number of Responses	Percentage of Responses
Information Broker	16	20
Information Specialist	24	30
Free-Lance Librarian	2	2
Library Consultant	10	12
President	7	9
Manager	2	2
Information Consultant	2	2
Other	18	22

appropriate terminology is because this type of information industry is in the developing stage and has not found its own identity yet. In their research, Gupta, Kundra, and Gupta (1983) indicates that the preferre d title is information broker. Other studies are equally inconsistent in using the various titles, and most list more than one title in the text of the article if not in the title. Two of the more creative titles suggested in this survey were information guru and information artist.

In a 1985 interview with Betty Eddison, she described the original Warner-Eddison, established in 1973, as a "Full Service Information Company" and stated that the term "information broker" did not exist at that time. She explained her belief that "information broker" is misleading since a broker is one who acts as a go-between in putting two things together. She suggested using more descriptive phrases such as Research Services or Information Management Consultants (Pemberton & Gordon, 1986, p. 14).

It is interesting to note that 6 people declined to answer the survey because they did not believe themselves to be information brokers although the description of their services matched those traditionally offered by information brokers. Several other respondents replied in much the same manner, but they completed the questionnaire anyway. Notwithstanding the above, it should be noted that 32% of the respondents chose a title with information in its form, whereas only 14% chose a title with librarian in it.

Table 5 indicates the employment commitment of the surveyed information brokers.

The largest percentage of information brokers participating in the survey–77%–are employed full-time. The remainder either work only part time or work part-time in addition to other regular full-time employment. A number of respondents reported that they began information brokering as a second, part-time job, built up a client base, then began brokering on a full-time basis.

Table 6 reflects the satisfaction of information brokers with their income.

This question was deliberately left open-ended to provide for individual differences among the brokers and their perceptions of adequate salary, as well as to provide for living expenses associated with geographic differences. Sixty-seven percent of those surveyed felt they received an adequate compensation for their services, which is a positive indication for the future of this profession. Of the 27% who felt they did not receive adequate compensation, many indicated they were unhappy with some aspect of the business

TABLE 5. Time Devoted to the Business by Company Heads

Response	Number of Responses	Percentage of Responses
Full-time	56	77
Part-time	17	23

TABLE 6. Respondent's Satisfaction with Income from Business

Response	Number of Responses	Percentage of Responses
Receives adequate compensation	50	67
Does not receive adequate compensation	20	27
Sometimes receives adequate compensation	2	3
No response	2	3

already, and an inadequate salary accentuated this level of dissatisfaction.

It is interesting to note that fully 27% of the respondents felt their remuneration was inadequate, yet they continued to remain in the information brokering business and had been employed in it for five or more years. Furthermore, the majority of these individuals engaged in information brokering full time. A few of the self-perceived underpaid were still quite optimistic that their financial situations would improve in the future. It would seem that financial rewards are not the only reason for being in this profession.

Table 7 reviews the number of information brokers who have employees other than themselves.

Sixty-four percent of the survey respondents hire other staff either as regular employees who receive benefits, or as contract labor. Only 26% do not use any outside labor. The contract, or temporary employees were generally used for clerical-type jobs, such as filing loose-leaf services, or for jobs requiring a high-level subject expertise.

The data in Tables 8 and 9 illustrate the number of staff employed by the surveyed information brokers.

The majority of full-time staff (70%), excluding the company's principal, is under 5, while the next highest percentage (12%) is with firms employing over 50. There appears to be very little activity in the mid-range: companies included in the survey would be, by most definitions, considered to be either small or large, with the vast majority quite small.

Table 9 indicates the number of part-time staff employed by information brokerage firms.

Twenty-five percent of the businesses surveyed hired one FTE

TABLE 7. Other Staff Employed by Company

Response	Number of Responses	Percentage of Responses
Yes	51	64
No	21	26
As Needed	7	9

TABLE 8. Number of Full-Time Staff

Number of Staff	Number of Responses	Percentage of Responses
Under 5	28	70
5-10	4	10
11-15	2	5
16-20	0	0
21-25	I	2
26-50	0	0
Over 50	5	12

TABLE 9. Number of Part-Time Staff, Shown as Full-Time Equivalents

Response	Number of Responses	Percentage of Responses
.05	4	14
.75	2	7
1.00	7	25
1.50	1	3
2.00	6	21
2.50	1	3
3.00	3	11
4 or more	4	14

(Full-Time Equivalents), while 21% had two FTEs. According to the individual comments received, these employees acted as contract labor and were paid hourly wages without benefits. They were sometimes used consistently, with a set schedule, but most often they were hired to participate in a specific project or on an "as needed" basis. In addition, part-time non-professional staff were routinely used to copy articles, do filing and other clerical duties.

Overall, the staffs of information brokerage firms are quite small and operationally the firms would be classed as small businesses. According to questionnaire respondents, most began and remain sole proprietors who do the marketing as well as providing the services. Balancing their time in this manner might explain why

their companies usually remain small since their time would probably not permit supervision.

Table 10 demonstrates the level of education of the information brokers surveyed.

A surprising 81% of the survey's respondents had an M.L.S. degree, considering especially the emphasis on information in the titles, as indicated earlier. Most of them not only had the degree, but also had several years' experience working in a traditional library environment. This educational level is consistent with White's findings (1981) which stated that "most information brokerages are run by librarians who moved into it because of budget constraints of their former employers. . . . " With very few exceptions these information brokers expressed their belief that their success was largely due to their previous library and/or business experience.

Table 11 presents the various services offered by information brokers.

A full 88% of questionnaire respondents offer "research" as a service. This probably includes both manual and online searching. Consulting, online searching, and document delivery were each offered by 76% of the population and manual searching was offered by 75%. These findings are comparable with those of Maranjian and Boss (1980), whose study indicated 78% of information brokers offered manual searching, 65% did online searching, 85% engaged in consulting, 75% offered document delivery, and 84% provided research services (p. 48). Broadbent and Kelson (1984) also reported that research was high on the list of services offered by information brokers, but information-on-demand was higher (66% in this study listed information on demand as a service offered). Their respondents rated online searching higher than manual searching, and 80% offered current awareness, report writing, and consulting (p. 18).

TABLE 10. Training for the Information Brokering Profession

Response	Number of Responses	Percentage of Responses
M.L.S. degree	39	81
M.B.A. degree	9	19

TABLE 11. Services Offered by Information Brokers

Services	Number of Responses	Percentage of Respondents Offering Service
Analytical reports	19	26
Bibliographies	47	63
Consulting	56	76
Document delivery	56	76
Indexing	31	42
Information on demand	49	66
Translating	13	17
Manual searching	56	75
Market reports	23	31
Online searching	56	76
Publications	24	32
Selective dissemination of information	41	55
Research	65	88
Lectures, seminars, workshops	28	38
Abstracting	3	4
Job placement service	3	4
Cataloging	2	3
Library acquisitions	2	3

Broadbent and Kelson (1984) further indicated that individual information brokers rated in-depth research a high priority in services offered while information brokerage businesses rated information-on-demand higher. Participants in this study rated online searching higher than manual searching. Four out of five of the information brokers surveyed in this study offered current awareness services, consulting, and report writing. Three out of five surveyed offered preparation of bibliographies, document delivery, and organizing libraries as services (p. 18).

Thirty-one percent of the respondents offered preparation of market reports as a service, and it was noted that this area is extremely lucrative. One person surveyed offers market reports exclusively, and charges accordingly for this highly specialized service. At least one company prepares market reports for clients and later, with permission from the client, repackages them for sale to the general public.

Only 4% of those surveyed offer abstracting services. This can probably be explained by the vast number of abstracting services available both in print and online. Using an existing service would be much more cost-effective than doing original abstracting.

Cataloging is another low-interest item, being offered by only 3% of the information brokers surveyed. Manual cataloging is extremely time-consuming and consequently expensive. With utilities such as OCLC readily available and the ability to purchase card sets and spine labels through a variety of vendors, cataloging is not a particularly attractive service to offer, nor would it be lucrative.

· Table 12 indicates the monthly work-load handled by information brokerage firms.

Fifty-two percent of information brokerage firms polled received under 50 requests a month. The number includes a great variety of requests: major research projects, consulting jobs, single research requests, and items for document delivery. According to Maranjian and Boss (1980), most companies in their study averaged about 100 requests a month, with document delivery being counted separately (p. 18). These data cannot be compared because some respondents

TABLE 12. Number of Requests Received Monthly

Response	Number of Responses	Percentage of Responses
No Response	14	22
Difficult to Estimate	2	3
Under 50	33	52
51- 100	5	8
101- 300	0	0
301- 500	2	3
501- 800	1	1
801-1,000	1	1
1,001-2,000	2	3
2,001-5,000	2	3
5,001-6,000	1	1

in this study indicated their answers reflected only new business: they were not including repeat business or existing customers.

Table 13 identifies sources used to obtain information to fill customer requests.

Since extensive library/information holdings, whether books, journals, or loose-leaf type services, are extremely expensive to establish and maintain, it is not surprising that 76% of information brokers surveyed for this study use libraries as their primary resources. Nor is it surprising that 73% rely heavily on online databases which are readily available in myriad subject areas. This parallels the study by Maranjian and Boss (1980) which indicated that nearby libraries and online databases were used more than half the time to fill client requests. Other sources cited for use included government, distant libraries, staff expertise, and agreements with foreign information services (pp. 18-19). Broadbent and Kelson (1984) stated that libraries and in-house information were frequently cited as resources used, along with online databases. Information brokerage firms, as opposed to individuals in the business, rated "phone contacts" and experts in related fields to be their best resources (p. 19).

There is some controversy surrounding the use of libraries and library resources by information brokers. The writer feels this issue falls in the category of personal ethics. Since most libraries used by

TABLE 13. Sources Used to Obtain Information

Response	Number of Responses	Percentage of Respondents
Experts	27	36
In-house collections	26	35
Libraries	56	76
Online databases	54	73
Other information services	23	31
In-house databases	2	3
Authors/publishers	2	3
Government sources	3	4
Associations and trade specialists	3	4

information brokers are public or university and are supported by public funds, these facilities should continue to be available for use by information brokers if they act in a responsible manner: paying royalties, if necessary, and not using library staff, for example.

Table 14 summarizes assumption of legal responsibility by the information brokers reporting in this study.

An overwhelming 85% of the respondents in this study do not assume any legal responsibility for information they provide to clients. Many indicated that liability insurance is out of the question because it is prohibitively expensive. Several provide written disclaimers in their contracts with clients and/or in their advertising literature. Others simply do not address the issue at all. This finding is consistent with that of Maranjian and Boss (1980) who found only one service which assumed legal liability for providing accurate information. Most respondents in their study felt that providing, information from secondary sources did not constitute a concern for liability (p. 19). White (1980) also substantiates this in stating that most brokerages "restrict themselves to the provision of publicly available information and some print a disclaimer in their brochures" (p. 14).

Table 15 shows the perception of the respondents concerning the future of information brokering.

Although 61% of information brokers polled believed that the business as a whole has growth potential, many were somewhat restrained in their enthusiasm. The majority, however, were very positive in their outlook for the industry. Only 7% were completely negative about the future of the business, while 14% felt there would be little change one way or the other. The most often expressed concern was the increasing availability and promotion of products to potential online end-users. Many felt this poses a tan-

TABLE 14. Assumption of Legal Responsibility

Response	Number of Responses	Percentage of Responses
Yes	10	15
No	58	85

TABLE 15. Future of Brokering

Response	Number of Responses	Percentage of Responses
Positive	40	61
Negative	5	7
Status Quo	9	14
Neutral	12	18

gible threat to the growth of the information brokering business, even to the point of threatening existing business. Others viewed this as a small problem, indicating that end-users might not have the time or the desire to do their own online searching.

Maranjian and Boss echo this concern when they state that "the industry is not only vulnerable to a possible increase in client sophistication, but also to changes in technology. This is especially true of the segment that relies heavily on revenue from online searching." However, they further state that as more information becomes available to end users, there will be an increased need for validation, interpretation, and evaluation. Consequently, information consulting may be the wave of the future (pp. 125-126). Broadbent and Kelson (1984) state:

> individuals and organizations who provide information services on demand for a profit would seem to be here to stay and may be an expanding area for those with a background and experience in librarianship. (p. 20)

According to Rodwell (1987), "fee-based client-oriented services will have a significant place in the future information marketplace" (p. 105).

RESULTS FROM THE INTERVIEWS

Questionnaires were sent to 125 information brokers identified in *The Directory of Fee-Based Services* as having been in business for a minimum of five years and offering diversified service to their clients. The responses of the 79 completed and returned questionnaires were analyzed and six participants were chosen to complete a more detailed survey based on the following criteria:

1. The respondent had to be the original principal in the firm.
2. The respondent had to hold an M.L.S. degree.
3. The respondent had to feel that he/she was adequately compensated by the business.
4. The business had to provide full-time employment for the principal.
5. Size of the company: two each were chosen to represent small firms (1 to 5 employees), medium firms (6 to 25 employees), and large firms (26 or more employees).

Actual results from the interviews are given in the Appendices. The following information was synthesized from the responses of the interviewees.

Of the six information brokerage firms selected to participate in the detailed survey, half (3) were established in 1982. The other three were established in 1974, 1977, and 1980. One-third (2) were begun by a principal with a partner, and only one still has the partner; two-thirds (4) were started solely by the principal of the company. Five of the six companies are currently structured as corporations; one remains as a sole proprietorship. All six principals who participated in the study have an M.L.S. degree, two of whom additionally have a master's degree in Business Administration.

Virtually all companies provide research in the form of online and manual searching and consulting. All but one offer document delivery. One company heavily emphasizes records management while another offers employee placement services. Two companies specialize in law-related activities to some degree, one's interest is the energy field and another's main area is non-profit organizations. All six respondents use libraries and online searching to supply requests for information. Four out of six use other information services and in-house collections, and three refer to experts or subject specialists for information.

Only one company assumes any legal responsibility for its services/products. It is covered by commercial liability, bonding, and errors and omissions insurance. One company stands by the quality of its work, and one informs its clients concerning the accuracy of the sources used for gathering information.

As a whole, the respondents fit into the typical "entrepreneur" profile. There were a few deviations, but even that is normal, since few individuals match all characteristics for any type of personality. Of the six people surveyed, only one did not have a high energy level. All liked to have feedback, felt they used past failures to their benefit, and felt they had a high need for accomplishment. One out of the six did not view him/herself as a goal-setter. All felt they took the initiative most of the time, took personal responsibility, and knew when and how to ask for help. Five out of six felt they had an intense level of determination, liked to see jobs to completion, and were problem solvers.

Propensity for risk-taking was spread out on the continuum: one person's rating was low to moderate, one was moderate, two were moderate to high, and two were high. The two extremes are somewhat out of character since most successful entrepreneurs fall into the moderate range of risk-taking. Additionally, librarians have not traditionally been portrayed as high risk takers.

Another surprise was the rating scale for level of self-confidence. In that rating scale, one was the lowest level and ten was the highest. In a business largely A concerned with public contact and selling, the perception is that people employed in such a manner would be highly self-confident. Although all respondents rated themselves above the median for self-confidence, none rated themselves a 10; three gave themselves a 9; other responses were 6, 7, and 8.

The most remarkable response measuring entrepreneurial characteristics was the question dealing with whether the person were motivated by money. The expected answer was an overwhelming "yes." The actual response, however, showed that one person was "somewhat" motivated by money, two were definitely motivated by money, but three were not motivated by money at all!

In the initial planning stages of the business, very few standard business practices were consistently followed. None of the respondents consulted a banker; all hired an accountant, and half retained a lawyer and developed a business plan.

None of the principals did a market survey to determine the need for an information brokerage firm in their geographic areas. Four had done moonlighting or had been approached by potential clients to provide a service/product. Two indicated their experience in the library field gave them a feel for what was needed.

Two information brokers began operations with no venture capital, one started with $5,000, one with $10,000, and in one case, both partners put in an amount of money: one went into the information brokering company full-time, while the other worked another job full-time and did information brokering part-time. Three respondents had no anticipated level of cash flow, one did not anticipate a profit, one expected to go in the red, and one planned to cover rent, taxes, and salaries.

In the first phase of the business, four information brokers purchased a computer, and two started with only a typewriter. One had a telephone answering machine, and one added a photocopier.

Only one person had a real core collection of materials–primarily directories, dictionaries, and encyclopedias. Another reported subscribing to professional journals. Two individuals have not expanded or established a core collection at all. The other four have increased journal subscriptions, reference books, and loose-leaf services.

One information brokerage firm began as a two-person partnership; one started with one partner full-time and the other part-time. The other four began as one-person operations.

In determining what services or products they would initially offer, one relied on "gut feeling" and client demand; one based the decision on understanding of potential clients based on 20 years of experience, one examined her own ethics and physical and mental capabilities. The other three offered services or products according to client requests.

Three companies offer new services based on client demand. One analyzes the service to determine time, energy, and expertise required to do it and how it will be marketed. After that is determined, advertising plans are laid out by an outside professional. This group develops a marketing plan every year–a very unusual process in this field. Another respondent, rather than analyzing the service or product, looks at her ability to carry it out. A third person interviewed finds out what the local competition is offering as a comparable service, then determines what anticipated costs will be in terms of money and effort. The existing client base is examined to estimate what volume of business they might provide for that particular service or product. Then the decision is made whether or not to actually offer the new service or product.

One principal decides to drop a service/product using the same line of reasoning. Another drops a service because it requires too much effort or because she lacks interest in doing it. Another broker discontinues a service/produce if it is not making money. If it is at least breaking even and bringing in clients for other services, it is retained. One respondent dropped cataloging services because it was too time-consuming and expensive for the client. Another response was that a service/product would be discontinued if it failed to meet the needs of the client. Even then, it might be modified rather than eliminated entirely.

The perception of the level of cooperation among brokers is highly disparate. Two indicated there is a somewhat moderate amount of cooperation, with brokers making occasional referrals to each other. Two felt cooperative efforts were high and two (both on the east coast) believed that cooperation among information brokers is low to non-existent because brokers are competitive, jealous, insecure, and/or profit-oriented. Some information brokers have cooperative agreements with each other–primarily informal agreements, but this is somewhat rare and not very popular. Information: brokers do charge each other for services provided, seldom offering a discount. The whole cooperation issue here is interesting. Librarians are trained to give information or to share it, while business practices dictate a profit orientation. It appears that the individuals participating in this study have, for the most part, successfully made the transition from non-profit, or not-for-profit, to profit.

Fees are established in a variety of ways, depending on the job. A few jobs are done on a flat rate. Document delivery is usually a flat fee which covers expenses plus a profit margin. Computerized literature searching is charged as a pass-along fee from the vendor plus an hourly rate for the searcher's time. One company bases its fees on what the competition is charging, while another bases charges on whether it wants or needs to increase or decrease business, what the competition is doing, and if the clients are in the public or non-profit sector. Most other services, such as abstracting, indexing, filing loose-leaf services, cataloging, etc., are charged by the hour which varies depending on the level of skill required for the task. Some information brokers give high-use clients special rates.

An issue which is of great concern to most librarians surprisingly seems to be of minor concern to information brokers: the problem of copyrighted materials. Two information brokers pay royalties through Copyright Clearance Center. One said it had never been a problem, and the other three respondents generally felt a client has the right to one copy of an article regardless of who makes the copy so they assume no obligation to pay royalties or to request permission to copy.

Most information brokers agree that advertising in the Yellow Pages and in newspapers is unproductive. They also agree that the best advertising comes from, word-of-mouth, from public speaking, and from being highly visible. Two indicated success with direct mail, while one found it to be unsuccessful. One frequently advertises in trade and professional journals; one never does. One respondent has been successful with radio spots played during commuting time on the easy listening stations.

Unexpectedly, only one information broker began business because of lack of available jobs after library school. Another was in a nonprofit organization which folded when federal funding was cut. One respondent with an entrepreneurial eye saw the need, felt she had the skills to fill the need, and pursued it. One woman felt she had nowhere to go in her organization; she was ready for a challenge, and with a newly acquired M.B.A., she saw herself as a marketable commodity. Two of those surveyed mentioned enjoying change and finding the information brokering field to be exciting. Two former librarians left traditional jobs due to frustration with those jobs. Both expressed the letdown of not being able to see a project to completion, not receiving feed-back, essentially not being able to perform at optimum capacity, and not being able to offer service of the highest quality.

The information professionals interviewed all agreed that the main advantages of information brokering as opposed to a more traditional library job are:

1. Excitement, change, challenge
2. Freedom
3. Ability to provide quality work
4. Receiving feedback
5. Lack of routine

One person had only pre-M.L.S. library experience. The other five had up to 25 years of professional experience. They had a variety of backgrounds: public, academic, and special libraries, with the greatest total amount of experience in special libraries.

The six interviewees attribute their success to a variety of factors:

1. Flexibility, openness to change
2. Vision–recognizing the need and filling it
3. Being able to deliver quality work
4. Drive, ambition, self-confidence
5. Putting the client first

When questioned about the effect of a depressed economy on the information brokerage business, one person did not respond, one felt the business was not affected at all by a poor economy, one believed the information business also becomes depressed. Three, however, expressed their views that a depressed economy is actually beneficial to the information industry. Where there is a reduction in income, special libraries are often cut back or eliminated since they are overhead. Information brokers can fill in essential services and/or provide temporary or part-time personnel at a savings to the parent company. Also, certain functions, such as records management and filing loose-leaf services, have to be continued one way or another, and these are other good areas that can be picked up by information brokers.

In essence, all six participating information brokers agreed about why people getting into the business fail.

1. They see it as a "get rich quick" scheme and are not prepared for the hard work, time, and effort required to become successful.
2. One-person operations are especially difficult because the one person must sell and do all the work, and that person often is not well-equipped to do sales.

3. They begin operations with too small a client base and/or inadequate capital.
4. They do not understand basic business principles, i.e., profits and losses; they frequently price their services too low; they tend to be too general–they do not have a clearly defined target market.

The six respondents were almost equally divided over the future of information brokering. One had reservations, but believed information brokerage firms would continue to exist, but the smaller ones might not survive. Two said information brokering would absolutely decline in the future, and three believed it will increase because there will always be a need for high quality information which cannot be provided by public libraries.

Chapter V:

Model for Establishing an Information Brokerage Firm

Several publications describe how to establish an information brokerage firm. The suggestions made by Warner (1987, 1988), Warnken (1981, 1982), Leach and Leach (1984), and White (1981) are valid recommendations. These ideas, along with information obtained from surveys and case studies of successful information brokers, form the basis of the following suggested model for establishing an information brokerage firm.

PERSONAL CHARACTERISTICS

Individuals best suited for this type of business would be high achievers, goal-oriented, like to have a challenge, and be aggressive. They should have a moderately high level of self-confidence and also be moderate risk-takers. They should seek personal responsibility, compete against self-imposed standards, and very importantly, like to see jobs to completion. Being motivated by money would not be essential, but having high ethical standards would be critical to this field. Other requirements for this type of operation would be a high energy level and a great deal of determination.

[Haworth co-indexing entry note]: "Model for Establishing an Information Brokerage Firm." Johnson, Alice Jane Holland. Co-published simultaneously in the *Journal of Interlibrary Loan, Document Delivery & Information Supply* (The Haworth Press, Inc.) Vol. 5, No. 2, 1994, pp. 47-56; and; *Information Brokers: Case Studies of Successful Ventures* (Alice Jane Holland Johnson) The Haworth Press, Inc., 1994, pp. 47-56. Multiple copies of this article/chapter may be purchased from The Haworth Document Delivery Center [1-800-3-HAWORTH; 9:00 a.m. - 5:00 p.m. (EST)].

47

BACKGROUND

An M.L.S. degree, while not providing the only acceptable education background for information brokering, would be a definite plus. The M.L.S. provides a solid basis for being able to find information in the most efficient manner. It also frequently instills a service-orientation as well as a code of ethics in the individual, both of which are critical in the private enterprise arena. A subject specialty would be another advantage. Although generalists still do well in information brokering, the trend appears to be increasingly in favor of specialization. This can be a factor in coexisting with local competitors. Experience in a library environment would be a necessary ingredient in successful information brokering. Although a few individuals have done well with little experience, the majority of successful information brokers have had several years of library experience, whether in public, academic, or special libraries, or some combination of these.

ADVICE

Advice would be available from the Small Business Administration (SBA) which issues a variety of publications tracing the establishment of any small business. Many local chambers of commerce sponsor SCORE (Service Corps of Retired Executives), a group of volunteers through the SBA who offer free advice to entrepreneurs and fledgling businesses. They help evaluate the need for a particular type of business. In essence, they help determine the feasibility of operating a business within the confines of the local market and the current economy. In addition, there are a number of small business groups attached to city governments and chambers of commerce which will guide an individual in the development of a small business.

RETENTION OF AN ATTORNEY

A reputable attorney could offer advice on local, state, and federal laws which might have an impact on the business. He or she could draw up contracts for use with clients as well as partnership agreements or Articles of Incorporation.

RETENTION OF AN ACCOUNTANT

This individual could give guidance concerning tax laws, social security/unemployment requirements, and set up an accounting system. In a small business, the owner may choose to handle all financial matters after the books are set up initially. An annual audit by an independent accountant may prove useful or may even be mandatory, depending on the organizational structure of the company.

ORGANIZATIONAL STRUCTURE OF THE BUSINESS

The company could be structured in any one of the following ways:

1. Sole Proprietorship. A one-person business where the owner has all the assets of the business and is personally responsible for all liabilities.
2. Partnership. Two or more persons who agree to do business together and share assets and liabilities, capital and work-load in a pre-determined way. If this form of business is chosen, it should be drawn up in a legal contract.
3. Corporation. The corporation is the business and owns all assets and liabilities. The individuals who work for the company are employees of the corporation, and its shareholders may or may not be corporate employees. Liabilities of a corporation do not affect the personal assets of the shareholders. Articles of Incorporation must be drawn up by an attorney for this form of business.

CHOOSING A NAME FOR THE BUSINESS

This would require some research since a unique name is mandatory both for identification purposes and to avoid legal complications if someone else has rights to that name. An attorney can offer guidance on this type of research. Some people choose to use their names, initials, or some form of their names in their businesses; others choose a descriptive word or phrase to allow potential customers to easily identify services or products being offered. As long as no one else has rights to the name, either form is acceptable.

TARGETING THE MARKET

Selecting a target market would probably be the most critical step in establishing an information brokerage firm. Many successful information brokers did not select a target market–it selected them, so to speak. In many cases, these information specialists were employed in regular library jobs and had opportunities to moonlight. At the point when they decided to take a risk by establishing an information brokerage, they already had a clientele they were able to take with them. In instances when this does not occur, the prospective information entrepreneur must carefully select the areas which appear to be ripe for the services offered by an information brokerage firm. Advice from the Small Business Association or SCORE would prove invaluable at this juncture.

A market survey might be sent to those businesses ultimately targeted as potential clients. The survey could probe what the information needs of these businesses are and if they perceive a need for information within the organizations. Target markets might include area special libraries which could have a need for temporary help, document delivery for items not owned in-house, cataloging, translating, help with special or rush projects, or highly specialized information in which an information broker might have expertise.

Target markets might be selected according to size of the company, particularly if the information brokerage firm is generalized rather than being subject-specific. Small- to medium-sized companies seldom buy information services or products, but the large companies, even those with libraries, do. Specialization is recommended for the greatest degree of success: an information broker with expertise in an area or even with an interest and willingness to learn about an area has a built-in target market and can actively pursue that segment of the market.

SERVICES

Nearly all information brokerage firms offer online and manual searching: research services, in general. A large percentage offer document delivery, compiling bibliographies, indexing, abstracting, and current awareness services. Others establish and maintain library collections, catalog materials, translate foreign language documents, and provide market research, and create databases among many other things. The services to be offered by information brokerage firms are almost impossible to describe, since they are varied, according to the experiences, expertise, and interests of the principals of the company and/or the outside contractors they have available.

It is not at all uncommon to start an information brokerage firm which offers certain services, then to add or delete services or products according to the needs of the clients. Flexibility is essential in determining the services or products offered to clients. In doing legal research for a customer, the need for filing loose-leaf services may become apparent and be added as a service. A customer may approach an information brokerage firm and request a new service—records management, for example. Then the principals must weigh the situation to determine if it will be profitable, if they can put the time and effort into a new project or skill, or if they can contract it out to someone else, while maintaining their own integrity at the same time. On the other hand, services or products that are not profitable may be dropped to the general public but may still be offered to a valued customer to maintain goodwill.

STAFF

The primary staff of an information brokerage firm is the principal or principals. If the principal of the business is uncomfortable selling, it would be wise to either contract sales out on a commission basis, or to at least begin in partnership with an individual whose strengths include selling. Another advantage to this is that one person can be selling while the other is actually providing the services. Otherwise, an information brokerage has to split his/her time between selling and servicing. This is a delicate balance, easily upset, which can lead to frustrating, unproductive time, or create insolvable time management problems.

As business increases, new services or products are offered, or subject expertise is required, contract employees could be used to supplement the work force. It is a reasonably inexpensive way to handle additional staffing needs, especially for temporary or sporadic projects, since payment on contract labor is usually on a straight hourly basis, with no benefits being paid. One major drawback is that since information brokering does not require a large amount of capital, a contract employee might stay with the firm long enough to know the clients and because of few loyalties to the firm, might break off, starting a new business and even taking some of the firm's existing client base.

CAPITAL AND EQUIPMENT

An information brokering firm could be established with very few capital requirements. Many businesses of this sort begin as moonlighting jobs, with the individuals buying necessary items while they are working full time. Then when they decide to go into information brokering on a full-time basis, they already have the equipment they need and, frequently, a client base already established. Whether the information brokerage firm provides full-time or part-time employment for the principals initially, they should have enough capital in reserve to meet personal living expenses, pay office rent and bills, supplies, and cover all associated expenses. Essential equipment in the early stages of an information business include a computer and appropriate manuals, a telephone, and an answering machine. Later a copy machine could be added as well as a telefacsimile if warranted by demand.

PRICING

The most difficult, and the most important, aspect of information brokering would be pricing the service or product. Three considerations in pricing are:

1. What the information broker's time is worth to themselves.
2. What the market will bear.
3. What the competition is charging.

An accountant's advice at this time could prove invaluable in determining how to charge for an information professional's time. Most services are charged on an hourly basis, depending on the job and the level of employee required to do it. Online searching is usually charged by the hour, with a minimum amount of time plus all costs of the search passed along. Having clients establish retainer accounts is convenient for information brokers. It gives them a certain amount of income to count on and allows them to offer lower rates to these repeat customers because the brokers don't have to expend time and energy selling. Charging flat fees may be an option in some situations, but unless a person is highly experienced in estimating time needed to complete a job, he or she stands a strong change of losing a lot of money. Hourly fees and pass-through charges often work best, and seem to be most commonly used.

MARKETING/ADVERTISING/PUBLIC RELATIONS

The best ways of becoming known or advertising information brokering business are:

1. Brochures should be polished products which convey an image of professionalism. They may be used in mailings or as handouts.

2. Calling cards should be handed out at every opportune moment. They can be very successful at bringing in business.

3. Direct mailing lists aimed at a particular population can be purchased or can be built by the information broker. A direct mail piece should look polished. It could include a brochure for prospective clients, or it could act as an announcement of new services or products to established clients.

4. Public speaking is a very effective advertising tool. Many organizations need speakers, especially ones that do not charge. At such events, the information brokerage firm and its services are described, brochures are available, and calling cards are distributed.

Speaking to college classes, especially in library schools, can be very effective.

5. Teaching classes can reach certain audiences. These might include library science classes and classes in research at community colleges or universities.

6. Participation in associations/organizations by information brokers who should go where their target market goes. If special libraries is the target market, they should attend special library association meetings. If the target is the energy market, however, library association meetings, for the purpose of recruiting clients, would be a complete waste of time and money. Local chambers of commerce provide many good contacts.

7. Radio spot announcements, aired during commuting time on easy listening stations, can have positive results. A dialogue between two people discussing information needs can be very effective.

8. Word of mouth remains the number one method of bringing in new business. Satisfied customers spread the word. Dissatisfied customers spread it even faster. This is where quality service and professional ethics count in a positive manner.

BUSINESS PLAN

A business plan contains many of the elements already outlined which can be incorporated into a formal document. It is a requirement of most lending institutions when outside capital is being requested; it can be of value to any individual establishing a new business venture. A business plan is the written document, or blueprint, including the purpose and goals of the business and how these goals will be met. Each business plan is highly individualized and requires time and effort to be successful. Advice from an attorney and an accountant could prove useful in preparing the business plan. A strong business plan should include the following key elements:

1. Executive summary
2. Definition of the business
3. Organization of the business

4. Qualifications of principals
5. Market for service or product and marketing strategy
6. Financial data
7. Long-range plans
8. Illustrations and back-up materials (Warner, 1987, pp. 29-30)

Warner details these elements in *Mind Your Own Business: A Guide for the Information Entrepreneur* (1987, pp. 29-48). Other sources of information for writing a business plan are:

New Venture Creation: A Guide to Entrepreneurship, 2nd edition, by Jeffry A. Timmons, Leonard E. Smollen, and Alexander Dingee, Jr. (1985).

Business Plans that Win $$$: Lessons from the M.I.T. Enterprise Forum, by Stanley R. Rich and David E. Gumpert (1985).

Business Planning for the Entrepreneur: How to Write and Execute a Business Plan, by Edward E. Williams and Salvatore E. Manzo (1983).

DECISIONS

Many factors must be carefully weighed before determining to go into information brokering as a career. The primary *caveat* is that information brokering is not a way to get rich quick. It can be rewarding, but it can also be demanding. Anyone contemplating making this a full-time profession needs to evaluate what the trade-offs are and how they would affect one personally. Long hours and great effort are involved in a successful business and not everyone can pay the price to ensure success.

CONCLUSION

High achieving, goal-oriented, aggressive individuals have a decided advantage in the field of information brokering. Having an M.L.S. degree is also of critical value, but the most important step in establishing an information brokering firm is that of developing a sound business plan following the steps previously discussed. With advice from reputable sources such as bankers, attorneys, and accountants, and with guidance provided by the Small Business Administration, a potential information broker can utilize the business plan to ascertain the feasibility of the business and to implement the requisite steps in setting up a company and be assured of some measure of success.

Chapter VI:

Conclusions and Recommendations

SUMMARY

The study population originally surveyed consisted of 125 information brokers who had been in active business for a minimum of five years. From the 85 responses received, six were selected to further participate in a case study type of interview which focused on their characteristics and details of how they initiated their businesses. A model for establishing an information brokerage firm was then developed, based on questionnaire responses and recommendations found in the literature.

FINDINGS

The findings of the study have been summarized in the following categories: general responses (from the original questionnaire) and case study responses: characteristics and business planning.

GENERAL RESPONSES

1. The majority of extant information brokerage firms were established prior to 1980 by one principal holding an M.L.S. degree.

[Haworth co-indexing entry note]: "Conclusions and Recommendations." Johnson, Alice Jane Holland. Co-published simultaneously in the *Journal of Interlibrary Loan, Document Delivery & Information Supply* (The Haworth Press, Inc.) Vol. 5, No. 2, 1994, pp. 57-60; and; *Information Brokers: Case Studies of Successful Ventures* (Alice Jane Holland Johnson) The Haworth Press, Inc., 1994, pp. 57-60. Multiple copies of this article/chapter may be purchased from The Haworth Document Delivery Center [1-800-3-HAWORTH; 9:00 a.m. - 5:00 p.m. (EST)].

2. The term "information broker" is still being disputed as a valid title after nearly 20 years of use.

3. Seventy-seven percent of the surveyed information brokers are employed full-time in that profession.

4. Regardless of whether or not they felt adequately compensated for their efforts, most respondents expressed continued interest in the area of information brokering, indicating that financial rewards were not the only reason for being in this profession.

5. Most respondents hire additional full-time staff either as regular employees or as contract labor. Seventy percent of those have under 5 employees; 12% hire over 50 employees. Only 26% do not use any outside labor. Twenty-five percent of businesses surveyed hired one FTE (full-time employee), and 21% had two FTEs.

6. Services most frequently offered by the information brokers surveyed include, in descending order, research, consulting, online searching, document delivery, and manual searching.

7. Slightly more than half (52%) of the population surveyed received less than 50 requests for services a month.

8. A large majority (76%) of information brokers surveyed use libraries as their primary resource for information. The second most used resource (73%) was online databases.

9. The majority (85%) of participants accept no legal responsibility for the information they provide clients.

10. Most respondents perceived the future of information brokering to be very positive with good growth potential.

11. Most individuals surveyed had several years of professional library experience.

CASE STUDY RESPONSES: CHARACTERISTICS

1. All respondents generally fit in the typical entrepreneurial profile.

2. The ratings of self-confidence perceived by the interviewees ranged from 6 to 9 on a 0-10 scale, somewhat lower than expected.

3. Money was not the impetus for initiating or remaining in the field of information brokering; frustration with the limitations and/or restrictions in traditional organizations played a more important role in those decisions.

4. Half of the 6 companies were established in 1982; the others began in 1974, 1977, and 1980.

5. Two-thirds of the companies began as a sole proprietorship; two started with a principal and a partner.

6. All principals who participated in the study have an M.L.S. degree; two additionally have a master's degree in business administration.

7. All six companies provide research via online and manual searching as well as consulting. Five offer document delivery.

8. Libraries and online searching are used by all respondents to obtain information for clients.

9. Only one company assumes any legal responsibility for its services/products.

10. The information professionals interviewed indicated that the main advantages of information brokering are excitement, change, challenge, ability to provide quality work, and lack of routine.

11. One respondent had only pre-M.L.S. experience; the other 5 had up to 25 years of professional experience.

12. The six interviewees attributed their success to flexibility, vision, providing quality work, drive, ambition, and self-confidence.

CASE STUDIES: BUSINESS PLANNING

1. The information brokers surveyed did not consistently follow standard or recommended business procedures in the initial establishment of their companies. They frequently relied on gut feelings or previous experience to make many business decisions.

2. Only one person began business with a core collection of materials.

3. Individuals participating in the study appear to have successfully made the transition from the typical non-profit library attitude to being profit oriented.

4. The issue of copyright seems to be of minor importance to practicing information brokers even though violations could have major implications.

5. Most respondents agreed that the best advertising comes from word-of-mouth, public speaking, and high visibility.

6. Responses from the interviewees, based on their positive and negative experiences, resulted in the development of a business plan model.

RECOMMENDATIONS FOR FURTHER RESEARCH

The results of this study raise several questions. It is therefore recommended that further study is needed in the following areas:

1. The legal ramifications of information provided to clients by information brokers.
2. The copyright issue concerning whether or not an information broker can act as a representative of a client and make one free copy of an article under fair use guidelines.
3. This study was limited to successful information brokers. The criteria of success included having been in business on a full-time basis for more than five years. A similar study could be designed to include participants who had been in business two years or less.
4. A survey should be done on librarians who moonlight as information brokers.
5. Finally, a study similar to this one should be conducted with librarians who entered the field of information brokering but left it.

References

Bell, D. (1973). *The coming of post-industrial society.* New York: Basic Books.

Broadbent, M., & Kelson, D. (1984, November). Information brokers in Victoria: Doing what, for whom, and how. *Australian Library Journal, 33,* 13-20.

Burch, J. (1986, September-October). Profiling the entrepreneur. *Business Horizons,* 13-16.

Burwell, H. (1987). *Directory of fee-based information services.* Houston: Burwell Enterprises.

Busha, C., & Harter, S. (1980). *Research methods in librarianship: Techniques and interpretation.* New York: Academic Press.

Davis, M. W. (1975, February). A quick guide to free lance librarianship. *Wilson Library Bulletin, 49,* 445.

Davis, M. W. (1975, February). Information brokers: Who, what, why, how? *Bulletin of the American Society of Information Science, 2,* 18.

Davis, M. (1976, March). New information professional Q's and A's. *NYLA Bulletin, 24,* 1+.

Doebler, P. (1973, August 20). Profile of an information buyer. *Publishers Weekly, 204,* 71-74.

Doebler, P. (1972, October 16). Seek and ye shall find. *Publishers Weekly, 202,* 39-42.

Drucker, P. (1962). *The age of discontinuity.* New York: Harper & Row.

Felicetti, B. W. (1979, Spring). Information for fee and information for free: The information broker and the public librarian. *Public Library Quarterly,* 9-20.

[Haworth co-indexing entry note]: "References." Johnson, Alice Jane Holland. Co-published simultaneously in the *Journal of Interlibrary Loan, Document Delivery & Information Supply* (The Haworth Press, Inc.) Vol. 5, No. 2, 1994, pp. 61-64; and; *Information Brokers: Case Studies of Successful Ventures* (Alice Jane Holland Johnson) The Haworth Press, Inc., 1994, pp. 61-64. Multiple copies of this article/chapter may be purchased from The Haworth Document Delivery Center [1-800-3-HAWORTH; 9:00 a.m. - 5:00 p.m. (EST)].

Felicetti, B. W. (1979, December). Profile: Andrew Garvin, President FIND/SVP. *Journal of Fee-Based Information Services, 1*, 9-12.

Feverstein, E. D., & Mishkoff, A. (1976). FIND/SVP: An idea whose time has come. Presented at Special Libraries Association, Denver, June 6-10, 1976.

Field, A. R., & Harris, C. L. (1986, August 25). The information business. *Business Week*, 82-86, 90.

FIND: Information on Demand. (1973, October). *Burroughs Clearing House. 58*, 30+.

Finnigan, G. (1976, February). Nontraditional information service. *Special Libraries, 67*, 102-103.

Finnigan, G., & Rugge, S. (1978, January). Document delivery and the experience of information unlimited. *Online, 2*, 62-69.

Fragasso. P. (1978, February). Warner-Eddison associates?! *Bay State Librarian, 67*, 7-10.

Galvin. T. (1973). *The case method in library education and in service training.* Metuchen, NJ: Scarecrow Press.

Gupta, B., Kundre, R., & Gupta, S. (1983, June). Information brokers. *Annals of Library Science and Documentation, 30*, 63-73.

Holmes, E. Company profile: Warner-Eddison builds centralized tools for accessing information. *Information world, 1*, 13.

IOD: Everything you ever wanted to know. (1985, June 3). *Sales and marketing management, 134*, 33.

Johnson, C. (1987, February 27). Information brokers: New breed with access to secondary research. *Marketing News, 21*, 14.

Johnson, M. L. (1987. Summer). Information broker: A career in scientific and technical information service. *Science and Technical Libraries, 7*, 3-9.

Kibirgie, H. M. (1979). *Information market: A statistical methodological study of the issues associated with fees and the use of information.* University of Pittsburgh.

King, A. (1985, December). Self-analysis and assessment of entrepreneurial potential. *Simulation & Games, 16*, 399-416.

La Forte, S. R. (1982, Winter). Information brokers: Friend and/or foe? *Public Library Quarterly, 3*, 83-91.

Lesser, F. (1982). Look into fee-based information in the San Francisco Bay area. *Tidskrift for Dokumentation, 38*, 12-14.

Leach, J. A., & Leach, L. N. (1984, Winter). Establishing a business: Fundamental aspects for information practitioners. *Library Trends,* 327-336.

Lunin, L. F., & Cooper, M. (1982, May). Secondary information services: Development and future. *American Society for Information Science Journal, 33,* 143-189.

Malchup, F. (1962). *The production and distribution of knowledge in the United States.* Princeton, NJ: Princeton University Press.

Maranjian, L., & Boss, R. W. (1980). *Fee-based information services: A study of a growing industry.* New York: Bowker.

Marchand, D. A., & Horton, F. W., Jr. (1986). *Infotrends: Profiting from your information resources.* New York: Wiley.

Naisbitt, J. (1982). *Megatrends.* New York: Warner.

Neufeld, M. L., & Cornog, M. (1986, July). Data base history: From dinosaurs to compact discs. *Journal of American Society for Information Science, 37*(4), 183-190.

O'Leary, M. (1987, November). The information broker: A modern profile. *Online, 11,* 24-30.

Pemberton, J. K., & Gordon, H. A. (1986, April). Database interviews Betty Eddison, Chairman, Inmagic, Inc. *Database, 9,* 13-18.

Porat, Marc U. (1977). *The information economy.* Washington, DC: U.S. Department of Commerce.

Profile: FIND. (1979, November/December). *Journal of Fee-Based Information Services,* 9-13.

Roach, S. S. (1985, Summer). The information economy comes of age. *Information Management Review,* 9-18.

Rodwell, D. (1987, March). Information brokers–a future in the information market place? *Information and Library Manager, 6,* 87-107.

Rubin, M. R. (1986, Winter). The emerging world-wide information economy. *Library Hi-Tech, 4*(4), 79-86.

Salton, G. (1987, September). Historical note: The past 30 years in information retrieval. *Journal of the American Society for Information Science, 38,* 375-380.

Timmons, J. (1979, November/December). Careful self-analysis and team assessment can aid entrepreneurs. *Harvard Business Review, 57,* 199.

Towle, A. (1954). The use of cases for research. In McNair, M.

(ed.), *The case method at the Harvard Business School* (p. 225). New York: McGraw-Hill.

Warner, A. S. (1975, February). An independent librarian looks at: Information services: New use for an old product. *Wilson Library Bulletin, 49,* 440-444.

Warner, A. S. (1987). *Mind your own business: A guide for the information entrepreneur.* New York: Neal-Schuman.

Warner, A. S. (1988, January). Information consulting–setting up the business. *Online, 12,* 20-24.

Warnken, K. (1978). Directory of fee-based information services. Woodstock, NY: Information Alternative.

Warnken, H. (1981). *The information brokers: How to start and operate your own fee-based service.* New York: Bowker.

Warnkin, H. (1982, February). Q's and A's on information brokering. *NYLA Bulletin, 30,* 1.

Warnkin, H. (1982). *So you want to be an information broker?* Chicago: Information Alternative.

White, M. S. (1978/1979, Winter). Information trader. *Library Review,* 206-208.

White, M. S. (1980, February). Information for industry–the role of the information broker. *Aslib Proceedings, 32,* 82-86.

White, M. S. (1981). Information brokers, their role in the provision of information to industry. *In* nationwide provision and use of information. ASLIB/IIS/LA Joint Conference, Sheffield, England, 15-19 September, 1980. London, England: Library Association, 257-264.

White, M. S. (1981). *Information brokering services in the USA: Report of a study trip, April/May, 1979.* London: NPM Information Services, Ltd.

White, M. S. (1981). *Profit from information: A guide to the establishment, operation and use of an information consultancy.* London: Andre Deutsch.

Yin, R. (1984). *Case study research: Design and methods.* Beverly Hills, CA: Sage Publications.

APPENDICES

APPENDIX A:
COVER LETTER AND QUESTIONNAIRE

Dear Colleague:

Under the direction of Dr. Bernard S. Schlessinger, School of Library and Information Studies, Texas Woman's University, I am conducting a study entitled "Information Brokers: Case Studies of Successful Ventures."

Your help in answering the enclosed questionnaire, which will involve approximately 20-30 minutes of your time, would be greatly appreciated. A stamped, addressed envelope is included for your convenience.

Please be assured that your answers will be kept confidential, and any data referenced from the survey will be reported anonymously. Selected respondents will be asked to participate further in an in-depth interview which will result in case studies.

Your cooperation in responding to this survey is essential to the study. In addition, I would appreciate receiving copies of any brochures you might have available.

[Haworth co-indexing entry note]: "Appendices." Johnson, Alice Jane Holland. Co-published simultaneously in the *Journal of Interlibrary Loan, Document Delivery & Information Supply* (The Haworth Press, Inc.) Vol. 5, No. 2, 1994, pp. 65-115; and; *Information Brokers: Case Studies of Successful Ventures* (Alice Jane Holland Johnson) The Haworth Press, Inc., 1994, pp. 65-115. Multiple copies of this article/chapter may be purchased from The Haworth Document Delivery Center [1-800-3-HAWORTH; 9:00 a.m. - 5:00 p.m. (EST)].

65

If you have any questions, please feel free to contact me. I look forward to hearing from you at your earliest convenience.

Sincerely,

Alice Johnson

SURVEY OF INFORMATION BROKERS

NAME: _____

COMPANY NAME: _____

MAILING ADDRESS: _____

BUSINESS TELEPHONE: _____

1. When was your company established? _____

2. Who initiated the establishment of your company?

    _____ a. self
    _____ b. jointly
             with _____
    _____ c. other
             name _____

3. What is the organizational structure of your company?

    _____ a. sole proprietorship
    _____ b. partnership
    _____ c. corporation
    _____ d. other (please specify) _____

4. What is your preferred title for your position?

    _____ a. information broker
    _____ b. information specialist
    _____ c. free-lance librarian
    _____ d. library consultant
    _____ e. other (please specify) _____

5. Is this your full-time employment?

_____ yes _____ no

6. Do you feel you derive adequate compensation in this business?

_____ yes _____ no

7. Do you employ staff other than yourself?

_____ yes _____ no

8. If YES, how many full-time?

_____ a. under 5 _____ b. 5-10
_____ c. 11-15 _____ d. 16-20
_____ e. 21-25 _____ f. 26-50
_____ g. over 50

9. If you have part-time staff, how many full-time equivalents do they represent as a whole?

_____

10. What training helped to prepare you for this profession?

_____ a. Master's in Library Science
_____ b. Master's in Business Administration
_____ c. other (please specify) _____

_____

11. What services does your firm offer?

_____ a. analytical reports _____ b. bibliographies
_____ c. consulting _____ d. document delivery
_____ e. indexing _____ f. information-on-demand
_____ g. translating _____ h. manual searching
_____ i. market reports _____ j. on-line searching
_____ k. publications _____ l. selective dissemination of information
_____ m. research _____ n. lectures, seminars, workshops

_____ o. other (please describe) _____

_____

_____

12. Briefly describe at least 3 typical projects you have undertaken.

_____
_____
_____
_____
_____
_____
_____
_____
_____
_____
_____
_____
_____
_____
_____
_____
_____
_____

13. Approximately how many requests do you average each month?

_____

14. What are your primary sources for answering requests?

_____ a. consulting experts
_____ b. in-house collections
_____ c. libraries
_____ d. on-line databases
_____ e. other information services
_____ f. other (please specify)

15. Does your firm assume legal liability for the accuracy of any information it provides?

_____ yes   _____ no

comments: _____

_____

_____

16. What new services are you planning to add in the future?

_____

_____

17. How do you perceive the future of information brokering?

_____

_____

_____

18. If selected from the respondents to this questionnaire, would you be willing to participate in a 1-1 1/2 hour interview either in person or by telephone?

_____ yes   _____ no

APPENDIX B:
INTERVIEW QUESTIONNAIRE

Company:

Date of Establishment:

Principal of Company:

Organizational Structure of Company:

Staff:

Background of Principal:

Services Offered:

Sources for Answering Requests:

Assumption of Legal Responsibility:

Perception of Future of Information Brokering:

I.   Entrepreneurial Characteristics

1. Do you feel you have a high level of drive and energy?
2. On a scale of 1-10, with 1 being the lowest and 10 being the highest, where would you rate your level of self-confidence?
3. Do you consider yourself motivated by money?
4. Do you like to receive positive and definite feedback?
5. Do you use past failures to your benefit?
6. Are you a goal-setter?
7. Do you believe you have a high need for accomplishment?
8. Do you see yourself as being in control of your own destiny?
9. Do you take the initiative in most situations?
10. As a risk-taker, do you perceive yourself to be in the low, moderate, or high range?
11. Do you seek personal responsibility?
12. Do you find yourself competing against self-imposed standards?
13. Do you feel you have an intense level of determination?
14. Do you like to see jobs to completion?
15. Are you a problem solver?
16. Do you know where, when, and how to ask for help?

II. Establishment of the Business

1. In the initial planning stages of the business did you:
    A. Get advice from a banker?
    B. Retain an attorney?
    C. Hire an accountant?
    D. Develop a business plan?
2. How did you determine your target market?
3. Did you do a market survey to determine the need for an information brokerage firm in your area?
4. What venture capital was required to start the business?
5. What was your anticipated level of cash flow in the early stages of the business?
6. What equipment did you purchase for the start-up of your business?
7. What was your beginning inventory in terms of core re-

sources such as periodical subscriptions, books, loose-leaf services, and software?

8. Have these core resources changed since the business plan?
9. What staffing was required when the business was established?

III. Miscellaneous

1. How did you determine what service or product your business will offer?
2. What steps do you take to develop a service or product before offering it to your clients?
3. On what basis do you decide to drop a service or product?
4. How long are you willing to continue with a service or product before dropping it if it's not profitable?
5. When offering literature searches to clients, do you synthesize information into a report for them or do you present them with bibliographies from which they select items of interest?
6. What is the level of cooperation among information brokers?
7. Do information brokers enter into formal or informal cooperative agreements with each other?
8. Do information brokers charge each other for services provided?
9. What associations are you affiliated with?
10. How do you set fees for your services?
11. Would you be willing to share a range of prices you charge?
12. How do you handle the copyright issue?
13. Are your employees handled as regular employees with privileges of benefits or are they hired as subcontractors?
14. What is generally the educational background of your employees?
15. What advertising methods do you utilize?
16. What advertising method seems to be most effective?
17. Why did you decide to initiate this type of business?
18. What is your work experience before you began this business?
19. In your opinion, what factors contribute to your success?

20. What do you see as the advantages of information brokering as opposed to a more traditional library job?
21. How does a depressed economy affect the business?
22. Many individual brokers are said to leave the business in a relatively short time after entering it. Why do you think that is true?
23. Do you feel information brokering will be more or less in demand in the future?
24. Do you have any additional comments?

APPENDIX C:
QUESTIONNAIRE RESPONSES

Company: A

Date of Establishment: 1982

Principal of Company: Owner

Organizational Structure of Company: Corporation

Staff: Employed on an "as needed" basis: consultants and subject specialists

Background of Principal: M.L.S., M.B.A.

Services Offered:
indexing
market reports
research
bibliographies
document delivery
manual searching
online searching
selective dissemination of information
lectures, seminars, workshops
business library services
information center development

filing subscription services
public record searching

Sources for Answering Requests:
consulting experts
in-house collections
libraries
online databases
other information services
local/state/federal government agencies/offices/records

Assumption of Legal Responsibility:
No liability insurance; we do stand by the quality of our work.

Perception of Future of Information Brokering:
Wide-open and needing structure, professional guidelines
and communication between information brokers.

I. Entrepreneurial Characteristics

1. Do you feel you have a high level of drive and energy?
Yes, but not always directed in the right way.

2. On a scale of 1-10, with 1 being the lowest and 10 being the
highest, where would you rate your level of self-confidence?
7

3. Do you consider yourself motivated by money?
No. Money isn't the highest priority. It's a PERC.

4. Do you like to receive positive and definite feedback?
Definitely.

5. Do you use past failures to your benefit?
Yes, indeed.

6. Are you a goal-setter?
Yes.

7. Do you believe you have a high need for accomplishment?
Amen!

8. Do you see yourself as being in control of your own destiny?
   Some days.

9. Do you take the initiative in most situations?
   I'm an idea-generator.

10. As a risk-taker, do you perceive yourself to be in the low, moderate, or high range?
    Half way between moderate and high.

11. Do you seek personal responsibility?
    Yes!

12. Do you find yourself competing against self-imposed standards?
    Yes.

13. Do you feel you have an intense level of determination?
    Yep!

14. Do you like to see jobs to completion?
    Yes, that's why I left the public library sector.

15. Are you a problem solver?
    Definitely.

16. Do you know where, when, and how to ask for help?
    I hope so, but it doesn't work 100% of the time.

II. Establishment of the Business

1. In the initial planning stages of the business did you:
   A. Get advice from a banker?
      No.

   B. Retain an attorney?
      Yes. He was the chairman of the board of the library where I worked.

   C. Hire an accountant?
      Only to set the books up originally and audit them annually.

   D. Develop a business plan?
      Oh, yes.

2. How did you determine your target market?

    It was a combination of factors. When I began, I had three clients who had come to the library where I had worked asking for referrals for moonlighters. When I left the library, the clients came with me; one in marketing, one manufacturer, and one businessman needing information for his client. I got their feedback and sounded out members of the Chamber of Commerce.

3. Did you do a market survey to determine the need for an information brokerage firm in your area?

    No. I read the literature on surveys that had been done nationally. I knew I'd have to do a lot of selling on a one-to-one basis.

4. What venture capital was required to start the business?

    Under $10,000.

5. What was your anticipated level of cash flow in the early stages of the business?

    I don't remember.

6. What equipment did you purchase for the start-up of your business?

    I already had an electronic typewriter with memory, a computer system and modem and a photocopier. I now have a telefacsimile machine and electronic mail.

7. What was your beginning inventory in terms of core resources such as periodical subscriptions, books, loose-leaf services, and software?

    I bought directories: government and business-oriented, dictionaries, encyclopedias, computer vendor information. (I use government information frequently—especially federal regulations and Bureau of the Census reports. There's a Federal Depository collection near here and I use that.)

8. Have these core resources changed since the business plan?

    No.

9. What staffing was required when the business was established?

> It was and is a one-person operation with the back-up of 24 consultants (specialists) available on a contract basis. They aren't researchers–they're in-the-field specialists. It sometimes saves a lot of money to consult them *before* doing a search for the proper formulation of the search. Also having a second opinion is often good. They're on retainers and are paid as subcontractors, as are other employees used for data entry, runners, and clerical work. I seldom have trouble finding part-time staff.

III. Miscellaneous

1. How did you determine what service or product your business will offer?

> My own ethical attitude and my physical and mental capabilities. Also, the data that's available; if it can be accessed we try to do it if it isn't unethical. We *never* do private investigative work; we never do school assignments. Local universities have DIALOG. From an educational standpoint it's best for students to sit down as a librarian is doing a search so they can learn something.

2. What steps do you take to develop a service or product before offering it to your clients?

> Sometimes a client initiates a request. I find out what's available from the competition in that area. I always figure out what my anticipated dollar costs will be and what price I'll pay in the way of my effort. I also look at my *existing* client base and determine what volume of business for a new service might come from them.

3. On what basis do you decide to drop a service or product?

> The same way.

4. How long are you willing to continue with a service or product before dropping it if it's not profitable?

It depends on what it is. You keep some services because they're good for client relations.

5. When offering literature searches to clients, do you synthesize information into a report for them or do you present
them with bibliographies from which they select items of
interest?

Both. Synthesizing information is not common prac-
tice for brokers. Brokers research data and clients analyze it. I categorize data; that which is most important
is presented first.

6. What is the level of cooperation among information brokers?

I'm willing to share any information, but I find there's
an intimidation factor among information brokers about
sharing with other information brokers as to what services we offer, what fees we charge, what vendors we
use, who's good, who's bad–none of that scuttlebutt,
never mind about clients. I think it's more a situation
where the average information broker is too insecure
at the moment to feel at all comfortable with sharing
information with a direct competitor. Special libraries
and public librarians are even more leery of information brokers–they're afraid we're taking business away
from them. Therefore, I do public speaking at a library
school, discussing how information brokering is com-
plimentary to other library services. As a direct result,
my relationship with other librarians has improved.
Before, I faced the green-eyed monster every time I
met a fellow librarian, and I wasn't even a "librarian"
any more.

7. Do information brokers enter into formal or informal cooperative agreements with each other?

Yes. We have informal agreements which we could put
on paper if we wanted. Another broker and I share
information on new software. She uses different database vendors so we swap. She uses BRS. I don't be-

cause I find the overlap too great. Also, 90% of the
time BRS is too limited for the kinds of things I do.
She also provides me information on organizational
activities I should know about.

8. Do information brokers charge each other for services pro-
    vided?

    With one person I charge only for actual costs. With
    another, the agreement is we give each other a per-
    centage discount. That way when we resell informa-
    tion to clients, we have the normal fees we would
    charge without hiking it up a lot because a second
    person did the search. At the same time we're both
    information brokers and we feel obligated to pay for
    that professionalism.

9. What associations are you affiliated with?

    AAIP (American Association of Information Profes-
    sionals), the Chamber of Commerce, Business and
    Professional Women's Club, a Technology Council.
    These are very effective for me. I am not a member of
    any library associations for a good reason: I don't have
    any clients there. I wouldn't mind belonging to SLA
    (Special Library Association)–when I first formed the
    company I did join SLA. I found the rivalry and jeal-
    ousy was hard to take during the first two years I was
    in business. That's not why I dropped out, though. It
    was because I had no strong library involvement with
    any of them–no common ground with them at all other
    than to make them aware I could supplement their
    resources, which actually rubbed them the wrong way
    because everyone likes to consider themselves inde-
    pendent. People feel very strong private loyalties to
    their own collections and it makes life awkward once
    in a while when they have to bite the bullet and ask for
    help from an outside source. I found working through
    SLA for that kind of exposure and supplemental in-
    volvement was not all that worthwhile. Instead I do it
    on a one-to-one basis. I am about to join the Law

Librarians because I do have a paralegal background (and have completed most courses required for certification). I have a large number of legal clients. I find the background helps me with banking, accounting, and some unusual marketing requests that take me out in the town hall or other government offices for information not normally available in other places.

10. How do you set fees for your services?

When AAIP was established, one major area of credibility we tried to accomplish was what services we would offer, how we would charge and what we would charge. We went around the room, and asked everyone to give a profile of themselves. One-third of them responded with dollar figures and the rest hedged by saying it depended on the job.

11. Would you be willing to share a range of prices you charge?

I charge by the cost of the search plus an hourly rate. I bill for computer time actually used with a 15 minute minimum with increments of one minute thereafter. This means it usually costs my clients a minimum of $50. I do bid on some jobs in bulk.

12. How do you handle the copyright issue?

A person has a right to make one copy of an article for himself. My client is asking for that one article. I've paid royalties when I did the search–it's built into the base. If the client needs more than one copy, I make my contribution to the clearinghouse.

13. Are your employees handled as regular employees with privileges or benefits or are they hired as subcontractors?

N/A.

14. What is generally the educational background of your employees?

N/A.

15. What advertising methods do you utilize?

I sing and tapdance a lot. Public speaking to business classes at the various universities. I'm very active in the Chamber of Commerce. Periodically I do mailings to clients describing my services. I have done radio ads, newspaper and trade journal ads.

16. What advertising method seems to be most effective?

No paper ads have worked at all. I've done 10 second radio spots on "easy listening" stations which have been very effective. The spots feature two people discussing a problem one needed a solution to by tomorrow. The other one responds, "Well, I would call _____." I ran this during commuter time ten times a week for a month in March.

17. Why did you decide to initiate this type of business?

Frustration. I like to follow something through. In libraries you can make suggestions for finding information, but you don't get the feedback on results in the library environment. Now the feedback is direct.

18. What is your work experience before you began this business?

Public, Special and Academic Libraries.

19. In your opinion, what factors contribute to your success?

I always put the client first.

20. What do you see as the advantages of information brokering as opposed to a more traditional library job?

1. Feedback.
2. Satisfaction of being a quality control officer of information distributed to clients.
3. Enjoyment in negotiating with clients.

21. How does a depressed economy affect the business?

N/A.

22. Many individual brokers are said to leave the business in a relatively short time after entering it. Why do you think that is true?

1. They don't like sales and they must have sales,
2. they end up working harder than they expected to (if they have any business),
3. they get frustrated if they don't get clients,
4. they don't make as much money as they thought they would, and
5. they don't have business skills.

23. Do you feel information brokering will be more or less in demand in the future?

    More. We're expecting a broader client base. The issue is really the quality of the broker. Many are too casual. Businessmen don't have the resources at hand to get information and public libraries can't provide services–brokers are needed.

24. Do you have any additional comments?

    Many library schools are offering courses in information brokering. They're going about it the wrong way. They should recommend the person take certain business courses, sales courses, computer courses, and drop library science courses (except for reference). Information brokering requires discipline and a priorities list. If you don't have self-discipline you won't make it as an information broker. You must do sales. Be true to your client–keep your word whether it is verbal or written. Never do less than you say you will, never-take short cuts. Never charge more than you estimated.

Company: B

Date of establishment: 1982

Principal of company: Owner

Organizational structure of company: sole proprietorship

Staff: 1 FTE

Background of principal: M.L.S., 17 years of experience, online
    training
Services offered:
                analytical reports
                consulting
                market reports
                research
                bibliographies
                manual searching
                online searching
                lectures, seminars, workshops
                library development
                facilities planning

Sources for answering requests:
                consulting experts
                in-house collections
                libraries
                online databases
                other information services

Assumption of legal responsibility:
                No. Clients are educated concerning the accuracy of
                sources used.

Perception of future of information brokering:
                Dangerous, exciting, positive. It serves as a safety
                valve for the crisis the library profession is experi-
                encing.

I. Entrepreneurial Characteristics

    1. Do you feel you have a high level of drive and energy?
        Sporadically, not consistently.

    2. On a scale of 1-10, with 1 being the lowest and 10 being the
        highest, where would you rate your level of self-confi-
        dence?
        8.

    3. Do you consider yourself motivated by money?
        No.

4. Do you like to receive positive and definite feedback?
   Yes.

5. Do you use past failures to your benefit?
   Most of the time.

6. Are you a goal-setter?
   Yes.

7. Do you believe you have a high need for accomplishment?
   Yes.

8. Do you see yourself as being in control of your own destiny?
   Absolutely not. I'm just one of the actors here.

9. Do you take the initiative in most situations?
   Yes.

10. As a risk-taker, do you perceive yourself to be in the low, moderate, or high range?
    Low to moderate.

11. Do you seek personal responsibility?
    Yes.

12. Do you find yourself competing against self-imposed standards?
    Yes.

13. Do you feel you have an intense level of determination?
    Not really.

14. Do you like to see jobs to completion?
    Not always.

15. Are you a problem solver?
    Yes.

16. Do you know where, when, and how to ask for help?
    Yes.

II. Establishment of the Business

1. In the initial planning stages of the business did you:

    A. Get advice from a banker?
    No.

    B. Retain an attorney?
    No.

    C. Hire an accountant?
    Yes. We have two fiscal things going on here: the corporation (my marriage) and my business (free-lancing). We went to an accountant because of changes in the corporation. I probably would not have consulted him as soon about the business if I hadn't needed him for the corporation.

    D. Develop a business plan?
    Absolutely not.

2. How did you determine your target market?
    It was built-in. I was an employee under federal contract running a clearinghouse in a specialized subject area. The clearinghouse was shutting down because funding was cut. As part of my work I had set up resource centers and did research. The people I had been working with were appalled that the clearinghouse was shutting down, and were thrilled I decided to free-lance, so I had a built-in clientele and those clients have stayed with me.

3. Did you do a market survey to determine the need for an information brokerage firm in your area?
    It was there. My only problem was there was too much work in the beginning.

4. What venture capital was required to start the business?
    Five-thousand dollars the first year.

5. What was your anticipated level of cash flow in the early stages of the business?
    None. I didn't know what I was doing.

6. What equipment did you purchase for the start-up of your business?
    Phone, furniture and computer equipment, TI 1200 baud terminal and Osborne computer, printer, monitor.

7. What was your beginning inventory in terms of core resources such as periodical subscriptions, books, loose-leaf services, and software?

    Nothing; I had Wordstar, d-base II, and subscribed to Dialog.

8. Have these core resources changed since the business plan?

    I now have 50 periodical subscriptions and I buy books. I also receive review copies of books and software. The books are bibliographic and are concerned with library automation, librarianship as a career, paraprofessionals and microcomputers in libraries.

9. What staffing was required when the business was established?

    N/A.

III. Miscellaneous

1. How did you determine what service or product your business will offer?

    It was largely determined by my interest: health and human service, and I did things requested by clients. I allowed myself the freedom to work in many areas. Over a period of time I've come to a point where I feel I have to specialize again. It's getting too complicated; so many databases and so expensive. Now I refer to colleagues, and now there are colleagues to refer to.

2. What steps do you take to develop a service or product before offering it to your clients?

    I don't research the need as much as I research my ability to do it. If I can do the job at all, I can do it better than anyone. I can experiment without risking much.

3. On what basis do you decide to drop a service or product?

    I decide to drop it because I'm not interested in doing it. Automation, for example, because it's more effort than I want to put into it.

4. How long are you willing to continue with a service or product before dropping it if it's not profitable?

I make it profitable.

5. When offering literature searches to clients, do you synthesize information into a report for them or do you present them with bibliographies from which they select items of interest?

    I always synthesize when I have the option. At least I edit (I download) to weed out unnecessary material.

6. What is the level of cooperation among information brokers?

    High. I don't play with anyone who doesn't want to cooperate. I have meetings, we talk, and have a good time. I create an atmosphere of cooperation; I give a finder's fee, 70% goes to the person doing the job, 15% to the contract negotiator, 15% to me when I land the contract. Cooperation is decreasing. There's more cooperation on the local level, less on the national level.

7. Do information brokers enter into formal or informal cooperative agreements with each other?

    No.

8. Do information brokers charge each other for services provided?

    I pay people for their time when I want to learn something or want a second opinion.

9. What associations are you affiliated with?

    AAIP, SLA–A lot of them are clients and I get a lot of referrals from them. The local chapter is very active, ALA off and on.

10. How do you set fees for your services?

    By what I feel I need, how much business is coming in; whether I want to increase or decrease my business; what my colleagues are doing; who my clients are; I charge more for-profit organizations.

11. Would you be willing to share a range of prices you charge?

    Twenty dollars an hour for non-profit organizations

(long time contract)
Sixty-five dollars an hour standard fee.

12. How do you handle the copyright issue?

I don't do much document delivery. When I do I go through another broker. I talk to clients about the data-bases and about their use of copyrighted material–it's an educational function.

13. Are your employees handled as regular employees with privileges of benefits or are they hired as subcontractors?

N/A.

14. What is generally the educational background of your employees?

N/A.

15. What advertising methods do you utilize?

I do direct mailings, but only to people I've worked with to let them know about a new service. I've tried the telephone directory, but it was useless. I got unwanted calls. I never advertise in trade journals or professional magazines. I also use business cards.

16. What advertising method seems to be most effective?

The business card is my #1 form of advertising. I do a lot of lecturing–for free, for money, for honorariums. This brings in *lots* of business. Half of my business comes from people who have heard me lecture or teach. I take lots of cards, and when I hand out bibliographies they always have my name, address, and phone number. This type of low-key advertising works.

17. Why did you decide to initiate this type of business?

I wanted to learn about searching, computers; I could only do this free-lancing. I also didn't want to go with another library when the clearinghouse shut down. The profession was changing rapidly. It was very exciting.

18. What is your work experience before you began this business?

I began as a page in the junior high library in the 7th grade, and worked through the 12th grade. I ran the library when I was a senior. As a college undergraduate I did filing at the New York Public Library. As a graduate I worked for H. W. Wilson as an indexer for *Library Literature*. Then I was a Young Adult Librarian in Queens. I volunteered for a hot line and set up a women's center. This oriented me to information counseling and I learned to ask hard questions. I also had special library experience.

19. In your opinion, what factors contribute to your success?

Love of my work, delight with any sensible question. Determination to find an answer no matter what is involved. Enormous flexibility. Enormous intelligence, intuition and good listening skills. Good logic, patience.

20. What do you see as the advantages of information brokering as opposed to a more traditional library job?

There are too many restraints on obtaining information in a public library situation. As a broker, you can go anywhere for the information; therefore, there are no mundane restrictions. It frees your mind to think globally–it makes you a better librarian. "Information isn't worth shit if it isn't in the right place at the right time." As a broker, you're on the cutting edge of new technology, new literature. You can carve out a lifestyle that's right for you: work 6 hours or 60 hours a week. The disadvantages are stress, it's expensive (e.g., buying telefacsimile machines), it can be fiscally unstable, it's lonely, and you can judge yourself too harshly.

21. How does a depressed economy affect the business?

Non-profit corporations (my target market) did go through a depression. I had been making about $5,000/month gross. Within 30 days all contracts dried up. Initially it hurt, but other things came up. Brokers can keep busy with piece work while full-time people may be laid off.

22. Many individual brokers are said to leave the business in a relatively short time after entering it. Why do you think that is true?

> It's not the lack of initial planning, but a lot of people just don't know what it's about. It's not a "get rich quick" scheme. It takes time and experience to start. People don't understand balance sheets, about paying social security taxes, etc. They don't value repeat business–they do a poor job and rip people off.

23. Do you feel information brokering will be more or less in demand in the future?

> It's hard to tell. Dialog prices are getting very high. Only people who can afford CD-ROM can compete. Smaller independents may be left out in the cold. *Or,* there may be loose affiliations formed for survival. I think there will be fewer brokers.

24. Do you have any additional comments?

> The deteriorating quality of government sponsored databases is a concern. Bottom line: Have fun and learn!

Company: C

Date of Establishment: 1974

Principal of Company: Owner

Organizational Structure of Company: Corporation

Staff: 5-10

Background of Principal: M.L.S.

Services Offered:
> consulting
> indexing
> research
> document delivery
> manual searching
> online searching

> lectures, seminars, workshops
> information management systems consulting
> information audits
> software development
> records management consulting

Sources for Answering Requests:
> libraries
> online databases
> other information services

Assumption of Legal Responsibility: No

Perception of Future of Information Brokering:
> Status quo or declining because of tools (automated)
> which enable users to gather information themselves.

I. Entrepreneurial Characteristics

1. Do you have a high level of drive and energy?
   Yes.

2. On a scale of 1-10, with 1 being the lowest and 10 being the highest, where would you rate your level of self-confidence?
   6.

3. Do you consider yourself motivated by money?
   Somewhat.

4. Do you like to receive positive and definite feedback?
   Sure.

5. Do you use past failures to your benefit?
   Yes.

6. Are you a goal-setter?
   Yes, to a certain extent.

7. Do you believe you have a high need for accomplishment?
   Yes–contribution would be a better word.

8. Do you see yourself as being in control of your own destiny?
   Yes.

9. Do you take the initiative in most situations?
   Absolutely.

10. As a risk-taker, do you perceive yourself to be in the low, moderate, or high range?
    High.

11. Do you seek personal responsibility?
    Absolutely.

12. Do you find yourself competing against self-imposed standards?
    Absolutely–too much.

13. Do you feel you have an intense level of determination?
    Incredibly.

14. Do you like to see jobs to completion?
    Yes. Not necessarily by me.

15. Are you a problem solver?
    No.

16. Do you know where, when, and how to ask for help?
    Sure.

II. Establishment of the Business

1. In the initial planning stages of the business did you:
   A. Get advice from a banker?
      No.

   B. Retain an attorney?
      Yes.

   C. Hire an accountant?
      Yes.

   D. Develop a business plan?
      No.

2. How did you determine your target market?
   Word of mouth–we didn't do much marketing initially; it was the energy market here.

3. Did you do a market survey to determine the need for an information brokerage firm in your area?
   No.

4. What venture capital was required to start the business?
   None. We worked out of our purses.

5. What was your anticipated level of cash flow in the early stages of the business?
   Neither my partner nor I had to work in the beginning. It was sort of a "tea-party" affair which became more serious as time went by.

6. What equipment did your purchase for the start-up of your business?
   Selectric Typewriter.

7. What was your beginning inventory in terms of core resources such as periodical subscriptions, books, loose-leaf services, and software?
   None. We used libraries in town.

8. Have these core resources changed since the business plan?
   We now subscribe to some journals; *Ulrick's,* union lists (local), *Books in Print.*

9. What staffing was required when the business was established?
   Two partners who did all the work.

III. Miscellaneous

1. How did you determine what service or product your business will offer?
   Our product offerings have been driven by our client needs, and we've been responsive to this. In the beginning our purpose was to set up and maintain special library collections in this area. Clients began to request articles not found in their libraries, and we grew into document delivery. That grew into research services, primarily in the energy field. Clients began asking us to organize their files since we organized their li-

braries, so we got into records management which we now do nationally as consultants. That business now dominates the business because you can charge a lot more for it, all businesses need it, and you can become more the hero for it than for library services by helping people retrieve their internal information more effectively as opposed to getting information from libraries (external information).

2. What steps do you take to develop a service or product before offering it to your clients?

None. The company has grown based on client demand. We've developed software for records management and one package for the legal profession.

3. On what basis do you decide to drop a service or product?

We've dropped our research service. We used to do a tremendous amount of manual research, especially in the planning area. We were able to make good money because we charged by the hour. Computer research has more hassle and less profit margin. I believe it will become so user-friendly everyone will do their own research. We refer research requests to a local library that has a fee-leased service. We don't encourage document delivery. We do that as a favor to existing clients.

4. How long are you willing to continue with a service or product before dropping it if it's not profitable?

N/A.

5. When offering literature searches to clients, do you synthesize information into a report for them or do you present them with bibliographies from which they select items of interest?

N/A.

6. What is the level of cooperation among information brokers?

There's a recent level of cooperation through the loose organization of brokers formed after SLA (Special Libraries Association). We get occasional calls from brokers wanting information specific to this area. The cooperation comes from a need for geographic information unavailable anywhere else. I don't see people referring business to another broker even though the other person may have the subject expertise needed for a job.

7. Do information brokers enter into formal or informal cooperative agreements with each other?

Some do brokering for other brokers. This business is so easy to get into, there's little loyalty among employees. They often break off into competitive businesses and that doesn't foster cooperation. There's an incredible amount of competition in the business, especially in research and document delivery.

8. Do information brokers charge each other for services provided?

Absolutely.

9. What associations are you affiliated with?

Association of Records Managers and Administrators (ARMA), Institute of Certified Records Managers.

10. How do you set fees for your services?

It's on a per hour basis for research, and per document for document delivery with the cost being determined by whether the articles were available locally or not. We pass-through direct costs (e.g., telephone, photocopy, copyright) except for computer searches. We add 20% to those charges.

11. Would you be willing to share a range of prices you charge?

For records management we charge $35/hour to $75/hour, depending on staff used for the job. For filing loose leaf services for lawyers: $15/hour to $20/hour; for putting books on the shelf, etc.: $15-$20/hour; library planning is higher.

12. How do you handle the copyright issue?

CCC.

13. Are your employees handled as regular employees with privileges of benefits or are they hired as subcontractors?

    It's a combination. Full-time employees have all benefits. Contract people used for filing, etc., are paid hourly, and their hours vary from month to month. I try to hire good staff people full time because of loyalty factors.

14. What is generally the educational background of your employees?

    At the height of offering library services, eight held the M.L.S. degree. We're now hiring a person with archival certification. We try to get people with a records management background, but Certified Records Managers are not readily available.

15. What advertising methods do you utilize?

    We've done some direct mail, but it wasn't very successful. We have a nice brochure and do public relations—talks, writing articles. We've also done space advertising and yellow pages, but both were unproductive.

16. What advertising method seems to be most effective?

    Word of mouth, giving talks, being visible on the national scene in records management, writing papers, participation in organizations.

17. Why did you decide to initiate this type of business?

    I couldn't get a library job after school—there was a glut of librarians in the market here at that time. I applied for a job which I didn't get, but the person doing the hiring called and told me about someone who needed a library set up. I did that for $5/hour and began to realize the need for that type of service. I got a partner and started the business.

18. What was your work experience before you began this business?

    Before the M.L.S. it was in the Arboretum Library at Harvard.

19. In your opinion, what factors contribute to your success?

   The ability to perceive where there's a market–willing to be open to change–flexibility. Recognizing the need for records management and software. We're honest–we deliver a quality product–a product that's worth the dollar.

20. What do you see as the advantages of information brokering as opposed to a more traditional library job?

   Library jobs are boring. Brokering is more challenging, interesting, rewarding; you can be more creative. There are not daily routines as in a library.

21. How does a depressed economy affect the business?

   It affects it significantly, especially libraries. Records management is less affected by changes in the economy. Special libraries are pure overhead, while records management (internal information) is always necessary.

22. Many individual brokers are said to leave the business in a relatively short time after entering it. Why do you think that is true?

   This is a cyclical business. If you have a sole proprietorship you work or you market: You can do both at the same time. People go into the business without specific knowledge for the specific industry. Most successful people have a specific market they're targeting and a specific area of knowledge. People are terribly naive about what to charge–they're too low. People are fairly naive about how much business is out there. People find marketing incredibly difficult. Generally people with information backgrounds are not sales types at all. Suppliers are doing a better job reaching end-users who use more time and therefore generate more money for the vendor, so there's less need for brokers. I think the areas where databases aren't available and information has to be gathered manually offer the greatest opportunities.

23. Do you feel information brokering will be more or less in demand in the future?

   It will absolutely decline.

24. Do you have any additional comments?
   We have no bibliographic control over special collections which should be looked at; they should be available through utilities.

Company: D

Date of Establishment: 1977

Principal of Company: Owner

Organizational Structure of Company: Corporation

Staff: 21-25

Background of Principal: M.L.S., computer training

Services offered:
   consulting
   indexing
   market reports
   research
   document delivery
   information-on-demand
   manual searching
   on-line searching
   selective dissemination of information
   lectures, seminars, workshops
   records management
   custom computer databases
   file systems
   cataloging
   library operations
   personnel services

Sources for Answering Requests:
   in-house collections
   libraries
   on-line databases
   other information services

Assumption of Legal Responsibility: No

Perception of Future of Information Brokering:
   The need is ongoing.

I. Entrepreneurial Characteristics

   1. Do you feel you have a high level of drive and energy?
       Yes.

   2. On a scale of 1-10, with 1 being the lowest and 10 being the
       highest, where would you rate your level of self-confidence?
       9.

   3. Do you consider yourself motivated by money?
       Yes.

   4. Do you like to receive positive and definite feedback?
       Yes.

   5. Do you use past failures to your benefit?
       Of course.

   6. Are you a goal-setter?
       Yes.

   7. Do you believe you have a high need for accomplishment?
       Yes.

   8. Do you see yourself as being in control of your own destiny?
       Yes.

   9. Do you take the initiative in most situations?
       More in business than in personal.

   10. As a risk-taker, do you perceive yourself to be in the low,
       moderate, or high range?
       Moderate to high.

   11. Do you seek personal responsibility?
       Of course.

   12. Do you find yourself competing against self-imposed stan-
       dards?
       No.

13. Do you feel you have an intense level of determination?
    Moderate to high.

14. Do you like to see jobs to completion?
    Yes.

15. Are you a problem solver?
    Yes.

16. Do you know where, when, and how to ask for help?
    No.

II. Establishment of the Business

   1. In the initial planning stages of the business did you:
      A. Get advice from a banker?
         No.

      B. Retain an attorney?
         No–not at the very beginning. I retained one when I incorporated.

      C. Hire an accountant?
         Yes.

      D. Develop a business plan?
         Yes.

   2. How did you determine your target market?
      It was experience. I knew the market because of 20 years of experience.

   3. Did you do a market survey to determine the need for an information brokerage firm in your area?
      No.

   4. What venture capital was required to start the business?
      None.

   5. What was your anticipated level of cash flow in the early stages of the business?
      I did not expect it to be profitable up front; I had a realistic business plan.

6. What equipment did you purchase for the start-up of your business?

    A typewriter and a computer.

7. What was your beginning inventory in terms of core resources such as periodical subscriptions, books, loose-leaf services, and software?

    Professional journals.

8. Have these core resources changed since the business plan?

    They've expanded.

9. What staffing was required when the business was established?

    Only one person in the beginning.

III. Miscellaneous

1. How did you determine what service or product your business will offer?

    It went with my understanding of my potential clients and 20 years of experience.

2. What steps do you take to develop a service or product before offering it to your clients?

    I offered services I felt had a market.

3. On what basis do you decide to drop a service or product?

    I would only discontinue it if it isn't meeting the needs of the client, then it would be modified or dropped.

4. How long are you willing to continue with a service or product before dropping it if it's not profitable?

    N/A.

5. When offering literature searches to clients, do you synthesize information into a report for them or do you present them with bibliographies from which they select items of interest?

    It depends on what the client wants.

6. What is the level of cooperation among information brokers?

    They occasionally do referrals.

7. Do information brokers enter into formal or informal cooperative agreements with each other?
   I haven't done that, but I do make referrals. I don't believe finders' fees work. I do it as a professional courtesy.

8. Do information brokers charge each other for services provided?
   Sure. I'd be a client. It does happen.

9. What associations are you affiliated with?
   SLA, ASIS, online users group.

10. How do you set fees for your services?
    Costs from vendors plus hourly rate of the searcher plus any direct costs.

11. Would you be willing to share a range of prices you charge?
    The pricing depends on the market.

12. How do you handle the copyright issue?
    Document delivery is a very small part of our business. We belong to the CCC (Copyright Clearing Center). We often buy whole issues of journals, and that takes care of the problem.

13. Are your employees handled as regular employees with privileges of benefits or are they hired as subcontractors?
    Employees.

14. What is generally the educational background of your employees?
    The majority have M.L.S. degrees. Some have master's degrees in subject areas.

15. What advertising methods do you utilize?
    Direct mail; advertising in professional newsletters and journals; advertise in programs at national meetings. We also have an exhibit booth at national meetings.

16. What advertising method seems to be most effective?
    They all work together–there's no one answer.

17. Why did you decide to initiate this type of business?
    I saw a need and had the skills to meet the need.

18. What was your work experience before you began this business?

    Special librarian, systems analyst, created databases. Twenty years experience.

19. In your opinion, what factors contribute to your success?
    There are three parts to a successful business:

    1. *Technical:* You're doing a job, doing it right and accurately
    2. *Financial:* keep up with income and out-go; good financial control
    3. *Marketing:* selling your product. If you combine these three factors you'll have a successful business.

20. What do you see as the advantages of information brokering as opposed to a more traditional library job?
    Libraries are *boring.* This is more interesting and more challenging.

21. How does a depressed economy affect the business?
    It depresses the information business.

22. Many individual brokers are said to leave the business in a relatively short time after entering it. Why do you think that is true?
    They have unrealistic goals and objectives, they may not have proper skills, they may need a bigger cash flow at first. People think this offers a lot of glamour—there's not glamour—it's only hard work: it requires a high degree of dedication. It's much more than a full-time job and many people don't want to work so hard. You should have a secure financial cushion.

23. Do you feel information brokering will be more or less in demand in the future?
    More.

24. Do you have any additional comments?
    When you have a one-person shop, you can't be an expert in all areas.

Company: E

Date of Establishment: 1980

Principal of Company: Owner and partner

Organizational Structure of Company: Corporation

Staff: Over 50

Background of Principal: M.L.S., M.B.A.

Services Offered:
> consulting
> research
> document delivery
> manual searching
> online searching
> lectures, seminars, workshops
> permanent and temporary employee placement

Sources for Answering Requests:
> consulting experts
> libraries
> online databases

Assumption of Legal Responsibility:
> Yes. Covered by commercial liability, bonding, and errors and omissions insurance.

Perception of Future of Information Brokering:
> No great increase in demand.

I. Entrepreneurial Characteristics

1. Do you feel you have a high level of drive and energy?
    Extremely.

2. On a scale of 1-10, with 1 being the lowest and 10 being the highest, where would you rate your level of self-confidence?
    9.

3. Do you consider yourself motivated by money?
   Extremely. If I weren't, I'd be working for somebody else.

4. Do you like to receive positive and definite feedback?
   I like to get any kind of feedback.

5. Do you use past failures to your benefit?
   Sure. You can't take it personally.

6. Are you a goal-setter?
   Yes. Your goals must be highly articulated if you're working with a partner/partners.

7. Do you believe you have a high need for accomplishment?
   Very high.

8. Do you see yourself as being in control of your own destiny?
   Very much so.

9. Do you take the initiative in most situations?
   Yes.

10. As a risk-taker, do you perceive yourself to be in the low, moderate, or high range?
    High. I don't feel I have a lot to lose.

11. Do you seek personal responsibility?
    Yes.

12. Do you find yourself competing against self-imposed standards?
    Sure.

13. Do you feel you have an intense level of determination?
    Yes. You have to. You can't be wishy-washy about it.

14. Do you like to see jobs to completion?
    Yes!

15. Are you a problem solver?
    Yes.

16. Do you know where, when, and how to ask for help?
    I'm learning to do that.

II. Establishment of the Business

1. In the initial planning stages of the business did you:
   A. Get advice from a banker?
      > No. New York bankers don't know much about *small* businesses. We read a lot about it first.
   B. Retain an attorney?
      > Yes.
   C. Hire an accountant?
      > Yes.
   D. Develop a business plan?
      > Yes.

2. How did you determine your target market?
   > Gut reaction. I'd been President of the New York Chapter of SLA (Special Libraries Association) and had gotten a lot of requests for temporary employees.

3. Did you do a market survey to determine the need for an information brokerage firm in your area?
   > No.

4. What venture capital was required to start the business?
   > We each put money into it. I kept my full time job. We rented an office and my partner came into it full-time. I came into it after 2 years. We didn't borrow any money.

5. What was your anticipated level of cash flow in the early stages of the business?
   > We had to cover rent, salary, employees' salaries, taxes.

6. What equipment did you purchase for the start-up of your business?
   > A computer; it's the best thing we ever did.

7. What was your beginning inventory in terms of core resources such as periodical subscriptions, books, loose-leaf services, and software?
   > None. We had Library Directories and resumés of people who wanted to work as full-time temporaries.

8. Have these core resources changed since the business plan?
   N/A.

9. What staffing was required when the business was established?
   We began with two principals. After two years we added clericals and later added more staff.

III. Miscellaneous

1. How did you determine what service or product your business will offer?
   Gut feeling–seeing what's needed; client demand, for example, document delivery.

2. What steps do you take to develop a service or product before offering it to your clients?
   We decide if we have the energy, time, and expertise to do something, who will do it, how we will market it. Then we begin to develop advertising: brochures, mailings, announcements. Someone does this for us. We do develop a marketing plan every year–our advertising person does this. Our approach is soft-sell. Ninety-nine percent of our clients don't need us at that time, but use us later.

3. On what basis do you decide to drop a service or product?
   We drop a service if it isn't making money, but we think twice about it if it's breaking even or bringing in clients for other services.

4. How long are you willing to continue with a service or product before dropping it if it's not profitable?
   Not long if it's losing money; longer if it's breaking even.

5. When offering literature searches to clients, do you synthesize information into a report for them or do you present them with bibliographies from which they select items of interest?
   N/A.

6. What is the level of cooperation among information brokers?
    There isn't a lot of giving. There seems to be the
    expectation that you'll *give* all your trade secrets.
    We're into this to make money. I'm not into sharing.

7. Do information brokers enter into formal or informal coop-
    erative agreements with each other?
    We do some document delivery for a few brokers for a
    high price. There is an amount of sharing–we make
    some referrals. We don't do large scale projects.

8. Do information brokers charge each other for services pro-
    vided?
    N/A.

9. What associations are you affiliated with?
    AIM, ASIS, New York Library Association, ALA,
    SLA, New York Library Club, New York Chamber of
    Commerce. The Chamber isn't productive, but it prob-
    ably would be in a smaller city. You should be active in
    local library associations.

10. How do you set fees for your services?
    We find out what the competition is doing. Our lawyer
    did some competitor intelligence for us.

11. Would you be willing to share a range of prices you charge?
    N/A.

12. How do you handle the copyright issue?
    It hasn't been a problem.

13. Are your employees handled as regular employees with
    privileges of benefits or are they hired as subcontractors?
    The permanent office staff and long-time temporaries
    get benefits: Most temporaries don't have benefits, but
    we pay their taxes.

14. What is generally the educational background of your em-
    ployees?
    All professional staff are librarians.

15. What advertising methods do you utilize?
    We use the local chapter SLA newsletter, SLA periodi-

cals, library periodicals in general. We do general and segmented advertising. We don't advertise our consulting at all–we just mention it.

16. What advertising method seems to be most effective?
     N/A.

17. Why did you decide to initiate this type of business?
     I had been in a special library for 25 years. I'd gone as far as I could go; I was ready to take a chance. The time was right. My partner was caught in a budget cut, we knew each other through SLA, so we formed a partnership. Getting the M.B.A. made me see myself as a marketable product. I saw I had skills I'd never use in my library. Also, we were impressed with Warner-Eddison and their operation.

18. What was your work experience before you began this business?
     I began working with the Army of Okinawa, then went with an encyclopedia publisher, two special libraries, New York Public Library. My partner has a variety of experience in public and academic libraries. The professionals working for us are from special libraries.

19. In your opinion, what factors contribute to your success?
     Drive, ambition, vision, self-confidence. Not being afraid of failure. "Pick yourself up, dust yourself off, start all over again." Being willing to take a chance.

20. What do you see as the advantages of information brokering as opposed to a more traditional library job?
     You get your own rewards–you have control over what you're doing. A real sense of achievement, you never know what's going to happen.

21. How does a depressed economy affect the business?
     When times are bad libraries cut back and need temporaries to keep things going and to reduce their permanent head count.

22. Many individual brokers are said to leave the business in a relatively short time after entering it. Why do you think that is true?

> There isn't that much need for brokers. If you don't already have a market, it costs too much time, effort, and money to market *and* do the work, especially for one person operations. Companies that see the need for information have a library. Information brokering looks good, but people try to start up with a too-small client base.

23. Do you feel information brokering will be more or less in demand in the future?

> Less. Companies can easily hire permanent part-time librarians. There are also problems with confidentiality. Brokers work from place to place which could really create security problems. I'm very concerned about this.

24. Do you have any additional comments?

> If someone wants to do something in an entrepreneurial vein, do it in a business-like way. You can't have a "librarian" attitude–a not-for-profit attitude. Use models from the business world, not the library world. Information brokering is a service business. You're better off learning how a service business is run, not how an information brokerage is run. You can't create a need if it isn't there.

Company: F

Date of Establishment: 1982

Principal of Company: Owner

Organizational Structure of Company: Corporation

Staff: 5-10

Background of Principal:
> law librarian
> on the job training

Services Offered:
>consulting
>research
>bibliographies
>document delivery
>information-on-demand
>manual searching
>on-line searching
>selective dissemination of information
>library management services

Sources for Answering Requests:
>in-house collections
>libraries
>on-line databases

Assumption of Legal Responsibility:
>No.

Perception of Future of Information Brokering:
>It will increase.

I.   Entrepreneurial Characteristics

   1.   Do you feel you have a high level of drive and energy?
        Yes.

   2.   On a scale of 1-10, with 1 being the lowest and 10 being the highest, where would you rate your level of self-confidence?
        9.

   3.   Do you consider yourself motivated by money?
        No.

   4.   Do you like to receive positive and definite feedback?
        Absolutely.

   5.   Do you use past failures to your benefit?
        Yes.

   6.   Are you a goal-setter?
        No.

7. Do you believe you have a high need for accomplishment?
   Yes.

8. Do you see yourself as being in control of your own destiny?
   Yes.

9. Do you take the initiative in most situations?
   Yes.

10. As a risk-taker, do you perceive yourself to be in the low, moderate, or high range?
    Moderate.

11. Do you seek personal responsibility?
    Yes.

12. Do you find yourself competing against self-imposed standards?
    Yes.

13. Do you feel you have an intense level of determination?
    Yes.

14. Do you like to see jobs to completion?
    Yes.

15. Are you a problem solver?
    Yes.

16. Do you know where, when, and how to ask for help?
    Yes.

II. Establishment of the Business

1. In the initial planning stages of the business did you:
   A. Get advice from a banker?
      No.
   B. Retain an attorney?
      No.
   C. Hire an accountant?
      Yes.
   D. Develop a business plan?
      No.

2. How did you determine your target market?

    It was there. I already had 5 or 6 clients when I started on a moonlighting basis.

3. Did you do a market survey to determine the need for an information brokerage firm in your area?

    No. I had spent 5 years with the Bar Association of New York library. That's where I picked up my moonlighting: these people had no one to take care of their small law firm libraries. I knew the market was there and it would just develop.

4. What venture capital was required to start the business?

    None.

5. What was your anticipated level of cash flow in the early stages of the business?

    It was a negative preconceived notion. I far exceeded it.

6. What equipment did you purchase for the start-up of your business?

    A telephone and telephone answering machine.

7. What was your beginning inventory in terms of core resources such as periodical subscriptions, books, loose-leaf services, and software?

    None.

8. Have these core resources changed since the business plan?

    I've added Martindale-Hubbell, reference books, and 2 computers.

9. What staffing was required when the business was established?

    Just me.

III. Miscellaneous

1. How did you determine what service or product your business will offer?

    My moonlighting started with filing loose-leaf services. Being a law librarian, I wanted to do more. It was a natural: my clients began relying on me more.

They asked me to give more service and I was willing to give it to them.

2. What steps do you take to develop a service or product before offering it to your clients?
   We don't give new services.

3. On what basis do you decide to drop a service or product?
   We've tried to ease up on certain things–cataloging, for example. It's terribly time-consuming and expensive for the client.

4. How long are you willing to continue with a service or product before dropping it if it's not profitable?
   N/A.

5. When offering literature searches to clients, do you synthesize information into a report for them or do you present them with bibliographies from which they select items of interest?
   Both, depending on the client and how our relationship is with them. Sometimes we do a search and give them the raw data. Other times they ask us to use our judgment and get them what they need.

6. What is the level of cooperation among information brokers?
   It exists.

7. Do information brokers enter into formal or informal cooperative agreements with each other?
   Yes. In AAIP there was much discussion on this. People will subcontract work out if they're too busy or if it's beyond their expertise. They are informal agreements for the most part.

8. Do information brokers charge each other for services provided?
   Yes.

9. What associations are you affiliated with?
   AAIP, American Association of Law Librarians, SLA

10. How do you set fees for your services?
    It's arbitrary–on an hourly basis.

11. Would you be willing to share a range of prices you charge?
    Twenty-$75/hour.

12. How do you handle the copyright issue?
    We don't do much copying for clients. We are acting as the company's librarian so law library management doesn't have any obligation concerning copyright.

13. Are your employees handled as regular employees with privileges of benefits or are they hired as subcontractors?
    With benefits, but we also use part-timers who are paid on an hourly basis.

14. What is generally the educational background of your employees?
    It's varied: college educated, down to high school. We have professional and nonprofessional services.

15. What advertising methods do you utilize?
    We do a brochure every 1 1/2 years or so.

16. What advertising method seems to be most effective?
    ———

17. Why did you decide to initiate this type of business?
    Frustration. I was tired of not being able to do the complete job in the way I felt was right. I felt stifled professionally.

18. What was your work experience before you began this business?
    Eighteen years in the law library field–mostly law firms. I did work in a library in an advertising agency for 3 1/2 years.

19. In your opinion, what factors contribute to your success?
    The high quality of the product.

20. What do you see as the advantages of information brokering as opposed to a more traditional library job?
    The freedom to work your own way and at a quality level. I think most people who go into brokering and stay, aren't in it for the money. They're in it for the career and personal satisfaction.

21. How does a depressed economy affect the business?

    I used to think a depressed economy was good for our business: the firms were paying for what they got and no more; they weren't paying benefits. But when the economy is good, many clients still need us, so I really feel that the economy doesn't affect us at all.

22. Many individual brokers are said to leave the business in a relatively short time after entering it. Why do you think that is true?

    They're in it for the money. They think it's easy. They aren't disciplined–they don't have the experience. There's so much they don't know and they're looking to make a killing right away. You have to make a living for yourself, but you have to do slow and deliberate things rather than just rushing in. I won't be a millionaire but I'll be comfortable and in control of my own destiny.

23. Do you feel information brokering will be more or less in demand in the future?

    More. There's always a need for information.

24. Do you have any additional comments?

    N/A.

KAPPA'S INTERLIBRARY LOAN WORLD

[Haworth co-indexing entry note]: "Kappa's Interlibrary Loan World." Waugh, Kappa. Co-published simultaneously in the *Journal of Interlibrary Loan, Document Delivery & Information Supply* (The Haworth Press, Inc.) Vol. 5, No. 2, 1994, p. 117; and; *Information Brokers: Case Studies of Successful Ventures* (Alice Jane Holland Johnson) The Haworth Press, Inc., 1994, p. 117. Multiple copies of this article/chapter may be purchased from The Haworth Document Delivery Center [1-800-3-HAWORTH; 9:00 a.m. - 5:00 p.m. (EST)].

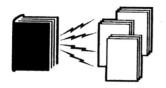

Haworth
DOCUMENT DELIVERY
SERVICE

This new service provides a single-article order form for any article from a Haworth journal.

- *Time Saving:* No running around from library to library to find a specific article.
- *Cost Effective:* All costs are kept down to a minimum.
- *Fast Delivery:* Choose from several options, including same-day FAX.
- *No Copyright Hassles:* You will be supplied by the original publisher.
- *Easy Payment:* Choose from several easy payment methods.

Open Accounts Welcome for ...
- Library Interlibrary Loan Departments
- Library Network/Consortia Wishing to Provide Single-Article Services
- Indexing/Abstracting Services with Single Article Provision Services
- Document Provision Brokers and Freelance Information Service Providers

---

MAIL or *FAX* THIS ENTIRE ORDER FORM TO:

Attn: **Marianne Arnold**
Haworth Document Delivery Service
The Haworth Press, Inc.
10 Alice Street
Binghamton, NY 13904-1580

or **FAX:** (607) 722-1424
or **CALL:** 1-800-3-HAWORTH
(1-800-342-9678; 9am-5pm EST)

PLEASE SEND ME PHOTOCOPIES OF THE FOLLOWING SINGLE ARTICLES:
1) Journal Title: _____
   Vol/Issue/Year: _____ Starting & Ending Pages: _____
   Article Title: _____
   _____

2) Journal Title: _____
   Vol/Issue/Year: _____ Starting & Ending Pages: _____
   Article Title: _____
   _____

3) Journal Title: _____
   Vol/Issue/Year: _____ Starting & Ending Pages: _____
   Article Title: _____
   _____

4) Journal Title: _____
   Vol/Issue/Year: _____ Starting & Ending Pages: _____
   Article Title: _____
   _____

(See other side for Costs and Payment Information)

COSTS: Please figure your cost to order quality copies of an article.

1. Set-up charge per article: $8.00
   ($8.00 × number of separate articles) _____

2. Photocopying charge for each article:

   1-10 pages: $1.00 _____

   11-19 pages: $3.00 _____

   20-29 pages: $5.00 _____

   30+ pages: $2.00/10 pages _____

3. Flexicover (optional): $2.00/article _____

4. Postage & Handling: US: $1.00 for the first article/
   $.50 each additional article _____

   Federal Express: $25.00 _____

   Outside US: $2.00 for first article/
   $.50 each additional article _____

5. Same-day FAX service: $.35 per page _____

   GRAND TOTAL: _____

METHOD OF PAYMENT: (please check one)

❑ Check enclosed ❑ Please ship and bill. PO # _____
   (sorry we can ship and bill to bookstores only! All others must pre-pay)

❑ Charge to my credit card: ❑ Visa; ❑ MasterCard; ❑ American Express;

Account Number:_____ Expiration date:_____

Signature: ✗_____ Name: _____

Institution: _____ Address: _____

City: _____ State:_____ Zip:_____

Phone Number: _____ FAX Number: _____

MAIL or *FAX* THIS ENTIRE ORDER FORM TO:

Attn: **Marianne Arnold**
Haworth Document Delivery Service
The Haworth Press, Inc.
10 Alice Street
Binghamton, NY 13904-1580

or **FAX:** (607) 722-1424
or **CALL:** 1-800-3-HAWORTH
(1-800-342-9678; 9am-5pm EST)